CHINA'S RISING
GLOBAL PROFILE

THE SUSSEX LIBRARY OF
Asian Studies

Series Editor: Dr Mina Roces, School of History, The University of New South Wales

The Sussex Library of Asian Studies will publish academic manuscripts in various disciplines (including interdisciplinary and transnational approaches) under the rubric of Asian studies – focusing on Economics, Education, Religion, History, Politics, Gender, and comparative studies with the West and regional studies in Asia.

Published

The Politics of Dress in Asia and the Americas
Edited by Mina Roces and Louise Edwards, *University of New South Wales, Sydney AND University of Technology, Sydney*

Chinese Identity in Post-Suharto Indonesia: Culture, Media, Religion and Language
Chang-Yau Hoon, *Singapore University*

Han Shan, Chan Buddhism and Gary Snyder's Ecopoetic Way
Joan Qionglin Tan, *Hunan University, China AND University of Wales, Lampeter*

China's Rising Profile: The Great Power Tradition
Harsh V. Pant, *King's College London*

Forthcoming

The Independence of East Timor: Multi-Dimensional Perspectives – Occupation, Resistance, and International Political Activism
Clinton Fernandes, *University of New South Wales*

Sports Media in China: Making Spectacle
Haiqing Yu
University of New South Wales

CHINA'S RISING

GLOBAL PROFILE

The Great Power Tradition

HARSH V. PANT

sussex
ACADEMIC
PRESS
Brighton • Portland • Toronto

2 4 6 8 10 9 7 5 3

First published in hardcover 2011, reprinted in paperback 2012, in Great Britain by
SUSSEX ACADEMIC PRESS
PO Box 139
Eastbourne BN24 9BP

and in the United States of America by
SUSSEX ACADEMIC PRESS
920 NE 58th Ave   Suite 300
Portland, Oregon 97213–3786

and in Canada by
SUSSEX ACADEMIC PRESS (CANADA)
90 Arnold Avenue, Thornhill, Ontario L4J 1B5

British Library Cataloguing in Publication Data
A CIP catalogue record for this book is available from the British Library.

Library of Congress Cataloging-in-Publication Data
Pant, Harsh.
China's rising global profile : the great power tradition / Harsh
    Pant.
p. cm.
Includes bibliographical references and index.
ISBN 978-1-84519-457-4 (h/c : alk. paper)
ISBN 978-1-84519-517-5 (pbk. : alk. paper)
    1. China—Foreign relations—21st century. 2. China—
Foreign economic relations. 3. China—Politics and
government—2002– 4. China—Economic conditions—2000–
I. Title.
JZ1734.P36 2011
327.51—dc22

                                                    2010041705

Typeset and designed by Sussex Academic Press, Brighton & Eastbourne.
Printed by TJ International, Padstow, Cornwall.
This book is printed on acid-free paper.

Contents

Series Editor's Preface   vi

Preface and Acknowledgments   vii

1 Introduction   1

2 China in the Asia-Pacific: Changing Regional   11
   Balance of Power

3 China in South Asia: Rapidly Expanding Orbit   29

4 China in the Indian Ocean: Challenging India's   51
   Geographical Predominance

5 China in the Middle East: Balancing the Applecart   66

6 China in Africa: The Push Continues But All's   81
   Not Well

7 China and the EU: A Relationship Adrift   94

Notes   104

Index   116

Series Editor's Preface

The Sussex Library of Asian Studies Series publishes original scholarly work in various disciplines (including interdisciplinary and transnational approaches) under the rubric of Asian studies — particularly Economics, Education, Religion, History, Politics, Gender, Comparative Studies with the West, and Regional Studies in Asia. The Series will publish emerging topics that demand attention in the Asian context — from the politics of dress to sports media in China, for example. Seminal works and approaches will find a home here. The Series also welcomes single-country studies or anthologies that explore one important theme across a number of Asian contexts. The aim is to contribute to scholarly debates on topical issues, highlighting the importance of the region to world economics and politics.

China's global economic clout has already been widely acknowledged. Harsh V. Pant's *China's Rising Global Profile* shifts the analytical lens to China's increasing engagement in international politics and expansion of its presence as part of the behaviour intrinsic to its status as a world power. This insightful and well-written account documents and evaluates China's emerging role as an important powerbroker in various regions of the world such as the Asia-Pacific, South Asia, the Middle East, Africa, and the European Union. The scope and breadth of this monograph makes it essential reading for all who are interested in mapping and understanding China's increasingly high profile role in contemporary world politics.

Preface and Acknowledgments

The spectacular rise of China over the last decade has shaken up the global geopolitical landscape and altered strategic realities, perhaps forever. China's influence is palpable everywhere these days, even in those parts of the world where the West and in particular America's predominance has generally been taken for granted. The genesis of this book owes to the vibrant debate across the world these days about the implications of China's global rise. This aim of the chapters to follow is to look at the presence of China in various parts of the world and gauge how that presence and corresponding influence impacts individual countries and regions as well as China itself.

Given the wide-ranging nature of Chinese interests across the globe today, no attempt is made here to be all-inclusive. Rather the attempt is to examine China's gradually expansive definition of its interests, its global engagements and the debate surrounding them as China stands on the threshold of making a leap towards the status of a 'great power.'

I would like to express my gratitude to Anthony Grahame who was instrumental in the transformation of a short proposal into a full-fledged book. I would also like to thank the Defence Studies Department at King's College London for giving me time to complete this project. Finally I am grateful to my family and to my wife, Tuhina, for their support in everything I have done so far. This book is dedicated to the memory of Guddi Mausi who passed away during this project and who will be sorely missed by all who came to know and love her.

To the memory of

Guddi Mausi

1

Introduction

After dramatically increasing its military expenditures over the last several years, China raised it by only 7.5 percent in 2010, marking the first time in nearly twenty-one years that the percentage increase was not in the double digits.[1] There are a number of reasons behind this development, but the Chinese government claimed that this change reflected its peaceful intentions, emphasizing that it has always tried to limit military spending and keep defense spending at a reasonable level. China's foreign policy thinkers and political establishment have long been trying to convince the world that Beijing's rise is meant to be a peaceful one, that China has no expansionist intentions, and that it will be a different kind of great power.

Of course, the very nature of power makes these claims suspect, and thus it is surprising that Western liberals have tended to take these assertions at face value. There is an entire industry in the West that would have us believe that China is actually a different kind of a great power, and that if the West would simply give China a stake in the established order, Beijing's rise would not create any complications.

But the domestic debate in China has moved beyond what the official rhetoric from Beijing might suggest. For example, one of the most prominent foreign policy thinkers in China has been advocating the creation of overseas military bases. Shen Dingli, a professor at Fudan University in Shanghai, asserts that "it is wrong for us [China] to believe that we have no rights to set up bases abroad." He argues that it is not terrorism or piracy that is the real threat to China. It is the ability of other states to block China's trade routes that poses the greatest threat. To prevent this from happening, China, according to Dingli, needs not only a blue-water navy but also "overseas military bases to cut the supply costs."[2]

Of course, Dingli wraps his suggestions in the standard rhetoric of world peace and diplomacy, asserting that the establishment of overseas military bases would promote regional and global stability. It is a familiar diplomatic wrapping that other superpowers should easily recognize. As China emerges as a global power, it will expand its military footprint across the globe, like other great powers throughout history.

In fact China's expansionist behavior has long been evident. China has been establishing naval bases near crucial points along Indian Ocean trade routes not only to serve its economic interests but also to enhance its strategic presence in the region. China realizes that its maritime strength will give it the strategic leverage it needs to emerge as the regional hegemon and a potential superpower. China has been quietly expanding its economic and political profile across the globe from its neighborhood in East Asia to far-flung areas in Africa and Latin America. It is this evolving global profile of China that is the focus of this book, which examines the growing role of China in various parts of the world: Asia-Pacific, South Asia, Africa, the Middle East, the Indian Ocean, and Europe.

Several themes emerge from the discussion in subsequent chapters. First, China's rise is a reality that can no longer be wished away. Its presence in various parts of the world is emblematic of its growing economic and military prowess and a concomitant expansion of its interests. Though China has benefitted from the extant international order underpinned by the US primacy, it would ultimately seek to change that order and shape it according to its own preferences. All great powers seek hegemony and China is no different. As John Mearsheimer argues, "there are no status quo powers . . . save for the occasional hegemon that wants to maintain its dominating position."[3] China's growing presence in far-flung areas of Africa and Latin America is a testament to its rising confidence in projecting its global profile. Worried about its energy security, China is already challenging the US in the Middle East by refusing to deal with the Iranian nuclear ambitions. In the Asia-Pacific, it is not only challenging the American primacy but also maximizing the power differential between itself and its most likely competitors such as Japan, India and Russia. Just as Sino-Japanese ties are becoming ever more contentious in East Asian waters, Sino-Indian ties are becoming problematic in South Asia and the Indian Ocean.

Second, the reality of China's global presence is much more complicated than many assume. The discussion in subsequent chapters brings to the fore the tough diplomatic choices that China is facing in various regions as it pursues its interests more aggressively. These include: projecting its soft power while at the same time paving the way for its emergence as a regional hegemon without sparking the creation of a counterbalancing coalition in the Asia-Pacific region; deepening engagement on a range of issues with a rising economic and military power, India, while at the same time preventing New Delhi from projecting its power beyond South Asia; exploiting natural resources while at the same time preserving its image as a benign global power in Africa; simultaneously courting both Iran and its regional adversaries in the Middle East; expanding its power projection capabilities in the Indian Ocean while at the same time ensuring that naval competition with other regional powers does not get out of hand; and preserving economic engagement with Europe while at the same time resisting demands from the Western world for political liberalization. How China manages to resolve these tensions will, in many ways, determine the trajectory of global politics in the coming years.

Third, much like the US, China is beginning to confront the costs of its rising power. The biggest kid on the block is rarely the most popular one. China's rise and its presence are not going unnoticed and unchallenged. Major powers are beginning to re-assess their strategic options. China's behavior is causing particular anxiety in the Asia-Pacific. The US policy-makers remain committed to maintaining their nation's primacy and will do their best to prevent the emergence of China as a great power. This will produce some inevitable tensions in Sino-US relations, affecting the entire international system. Hegemonic transitions, when a rising power begins to overtake the dominant one, have rarely been peaceful.[4] After suggesting that their nation intends to rise peacefully, Chinese political leaders are finding it hard to maintain that pretence. The myth of China's peaceful rise is being challenged by China's own actions as it expands its interests and asserts it power across the globe. Chinese restrictions on exports of crucial 'rare earth' minerals, first to Japan and then to the US and Europe in 2010, underscored for its trading partners China's propensity to use its dominant economic position as a political weapon.[5] Complaints about China's undervalued currency have only grown louder. China's lack of democracy is also emerging as a major concern. China is the only non-democratic power of the world's six biggest power and that will have profound consequences for the way other powers view China's rise. Meanwhile, China's neighbors are busy rejuvenating old alliances and reaching out to new partners to better defend their interests against the rising great power in their vicinity. Changing perceptions about China's rise were clearly articulated by Yoichi Funabashi, Japan's most important foreign affairs commentator, when in a letter sent to his high-ranking friends in China in response to Sino-Japanese tensions in 2010, he suggested that if China continued to undermine its "peaceful rise" doctrine, then "Japan would discard its naïveté, lower its expectations, acquire needed insurance and, in some cases, cut its losses."[6] In a way, he summed up the fundamental challenge that China faces as it continues its ascent in the global inter-state hierarchy.

A Spectacular Rise

China enjoyed average annual rates of real income growth of around 10 percent in the last two decades of the twentieth century, something historically unprecedented. China overtook Germany to become the world's largest exporter in 2009 and its share of world exports jumped to almost 10 percent, up from 3 percent in 1999.[7] China's share of world trade has continued to rise despite the 2008 financial crisis and it remains one of the most attractive destinations for foreign direct investment, absorbing more than US$90 billion worth of FDI in 2008. It has been estimated that by 2040 China's GDP will reach $123 trillion and it will account for 40 percent of the world's economic output.[8] China has already overtaken Japan to become the world's second largest economy, and according to various estimates, the Chinese economy may surpass that of the US by 2027. It is the world's largest recipient of foreign direct investment and holds more than $1 trillion in US government debt — which is only half of the foreign reserves that it has generated through its huge trade surplus and investment flows. China's state-owned enterprises are buying companies, technologies, and resources worldwide. China became the first major economy to recover from the global recession in 2008 and is playing a leading role in pulling the rest of the world out of it.

China is today an emerging superpower with growing economic and political interests in almost every part of the globe. The rapidity of China's rise to prominence around the world has surprised many, though it should have been obvious to those following China's economic trajectory. As China became economically powerful, it was bound to become ambitious and assert itself across the globe.

This is a trend that all great powers have followed throughout history.[9] China's foreign policy is aimed at protecting the country from external threats as it pursues its geopolitical interests so that it will be able to continue reforming its economy and thereby acquire comprehensive national power without having to deal with the impediments and distractions of security competition.[10]

For years, China had shied away from playing the kind of active role in international affairs that would seem commensurate with its economic importance. This was primarily because the Chinese political leadership had made a strategic choice of avoiding the potential distractions of interventionist international politics so that they could focus on domestic economic development. Deng Xiaoping had urged China's leaders to keep a low profile in foreign affairs. But the last few years have seen China abandon this reticence and signal that it would no longer be willing to watch events unfold from the sidelines, thereby accepting its new role as a significant global player. China is expanding its presence and deepening its engagement with states in all parts of the world beyond the Asia-Pacific, including Latin America, Africa, and the Middle East.

During the early years of the Cold War, China saw itself as being at the vanguard of the revolutionary communist ideology and devoted energy to spreading it throughout the world, particularly in the Third World. However, by the 1960s it had already become clear that this policy was a non-starter in most parts of the world. Though it tried to project itself as a leader of the Third World and provided support to several left-wing regimes, it was the former Soviet Union to whom these states turned if they needed support against the West. Given these challenges, China focused on developing ties with smaller militant groups, rather than state actors, settling on a policy that became known as the "radicalism of impotence" which gave China nothing substantive, but only propaganda advantages in the region.[11] With the end of the Cold War, China emerged as a major global economic player and other states started taking China more seriously. Meanwhile, China also started becoming more ambitious in defining its strategic agenda even as its primary concern remained global and regional stability, which were seen as essential for its economic development. Over time, China's foreign policy towards the Third World, despite its stated revolutionary aims, became evolutionary and pragmatic as trade became China's priority and other states became more tactful in their dealings with China, benefiting from its material aid and learning from its developmental trajectory.[12]

This newfound foreign engagement is also the result of a realization in China that an active international role is necessary in order to maintain its current economic trajectory of double-digit rates of growth. A significant proportion of oil and other natural resources needed to run the economy are imported by China, and so wooing nations that are rich in energy and other raw materials became important. Moreover, China also has to keep searching for new markets for its expanding manufacturing sector.

China is defending its interests in various parts of the world through the time-tested means employed by great powers, which include giving large amounts of economic assistance, subsidizing companies to help capture export markets, supporting governments that do business with it, and selling arms to regimes that might use them against their internal and regional adversaries.

China's mix of authoritarianism and rapid economic growth is attractive to states with fragile political and economic institutions and whose relations with the West tend to be ambivalent. China has deepened its ties with an array of autocratic leaders and military dictatorships in recent years including the Burmese military junta, Zimbabwe's Robert Mugabe and Sudanese Prime Minister Omar al-Bashir, wanted for war crimes by an international tribunal in the Hague. Beijing has begun to emerge as a political and economic alternative to the West in many parts of the world. Politically, China intends to build diplomatic support among nations for its priorities at the United Nations and other global institutions where its interests are increasingly diverging from the West. While not overtly trying to countervail US power by forming external alliances, China is trying to use "soft balancing" to contain US might by entangling it in a web of international institutional rules and procedures or ad hoc diplomatic maneuvers.[13] China's increasing engagement with the rest of the world also helps it to further marginalize Taiwan as the number of states extending diplomatic recognition to Taiwan dwindles in the face of the Chinese resurgence.

Not surprisingly, China is using all the levers at its disposal to raise its profile in far-flung regions of the world. China's trade surplus is mounting inexorably, as are its reserves of foreign currencies — the latter potentially of great influence in today's world. China is using its growing foreign currency reserves to cement diplomatic alliances, secure access to natural resources, and garner business for its companies even as it talks of a "harmonious world order" to counter the perception that a rising China is a threat. China has quietly reoriented its foreign policy to emerge as a new advocate of "soft power" — a combination of diplomatic outreach, cultural attractiveness and economic might that helps a nation persuade other countries to follow its lead.[14] Beijing is now even using its armed forces as an instrument of its foreign policy more effectively than ever before by maintaining military attaches in 109 countries, annually sending more than 100 military delegations abroad and receiving more than 200 visiting military delegations.[15] Joint military exercises with other states are helping in the modernization of the People's Liberation Army (PLA) as they provide opportunities to improve China's capabilities in areas such as counterterrorism, mobility operations and logistics. China's once suspicious neighbors have been drawn into its sphere of economic influence and it has been successful in extending its soft power to places as far apart as Southeast Asia, Latin America, and Africa, often as part of a quest for oil and other natural resources to fuel the Chinese industrial revolution. But gradually the costs of such a rapid expansion in China's global profile are also becoming apparent.

New Geopolitical Realities

China would not have expected that its arrival as the world's second-largest economy would also be accompanied by a new robustness in US policy towards China and the Asian region. The US Secretary of State, Hillary Clinton, used her visit to Asia in July 2010 to signal unequivocally that the US was unwilling to accept China's push for regional hegemony. When Beijing claimed that it now considers its ownership of the Spratly Islands in the South China Sea as a "core interest," Clinton retorted by proposing that the US help establish an international mechanism to mediate the overlapping claims of sovereignty between China, Taiwan, the Philippines, Vietnam, Indonesia and Malaysia that now exist in the South China Sea.[16]

Fears have been rising in Asia that China is seeking to use its growing maritime might to dominate not only the hydrocarbon-rich waters of the South China Sea but also its crucial shipping lanes, the lifeline of regional economies. And there were concerns in the region about America's commitment to regional security. Those concerns were assuaged by the US decision to undertake joint naval and air exercises with South Korea off the east coast of the Korean Peninsula in 2010. The US also underlined its commitment to freedom of the seas in Asia by undertaking war games in the Yellow Sea, despite Chinese threats.

At the same time, Washington has started making overtures to new partners in the region. The US Navy visited Vietnam in 2010 for the first time since the end of the Vietnam War. Building on their agreement to expand cooperation on peaceful uses of nuclear energy, the US and Vietnam are discussing a nuclear energy deal, with Vietnam deciding to augment its nuclear energy capacity significantly over the next two decades. Despite opposition from human rights groups, the US has announced rehabilitation of links between the American military and the Indonesian military's elite *kopassus* units, which had been suspended for decades.[17]

This new US assertiveness vis-à-vis Beijing has been widely welcomed in the region. The other members of the Association of South-East Asian Nations (ASEAN) strongly endorsed Clinton's call for multilateral commitment to a code of conduct for the South China Sea rather than China's preferred bilateral approach. For China, the issue was its sovereign rights and claims to the sea, whereas for the rest of the region the issue was freedom of navigation and respect for international law.[18] It was under American guardianship of common interests for the last several decades that China has emerged as the economic powerhouse it is today. Now it wants a new system — a system that only works for Beijing and does not deal with the provision of public goods or common resources. China's haphazard diplomatic approach and unnecessary bluster on South China Sea ended up exposing the myth of Chinese soft power in the region.[19]

Meanwhile, a day after China's economy was recognized as the world's second largest, the US Department of Defense in its 2010 report to Congress on China's military underlined the advancements the People's Liberation Army is making across the board in line with its burgeoning economic power. Beijing's military outlays are the world's second-highest and have tripled since 2000 to an estimated $100 billion in 2009 (though still well behind Washington's $617 billion). The results of China's military modernization program have been quite extraordinary: it now has the largest force of principal combatants, submarines and amphibious warships in Asia, one of the largest forces of surface-to-air missiles in the world, and the most active land-based ballistic and cruise missile system in the world.[20] The focus of China's military modernization program is on weapons that could prevent American warships from operating in international waters off its coast. But with the military balance in the Taiwan Straits tilting in its favor, China has set its sights much further a field as it looks to secure its expanding economic interests across the globe.

China's rise in the late twentieth and early twenty-first century is a return to the status it held for most of the past 2000 years, of East Asia's economic and military giant as well as the center of high-technology and culture. It should not be surprising then that Beijing has started dictating the boundaries of acceptable behavior to its neighbors, laying bare the costs of great power politics in the process.

The rise of China is now a structural reality that other states in the international system are trying to come to grips with. It is not only the extant global superpower, the United States, that has started pushing back. The Obama Administration has been forced to scale back hopes of working with the Chinese on major global challenges like climate change, nuclear proliferation and a new global economic order. It had come to office intent on making China a global partner in tackling global issues but found a powerful Beijing refusing to budge from its maximalist positions. As a consequence, the United States is now busy reinvigorating old alliances and shoring up its presence elsewhere in Asia.[21] China's neighbors are increasingly concerned about China's navy and its long-range ambitions, as well as China's growing assertiveness in the surrounding territories. The rapid and secretive expansion of China's military and its claims over almost the entire South China Sea is resulting in a galloping arms race among the regional states in the Asia-Pacific. Russia increasingly views China as the most potent threat to emerge in the coming years. After backing the Shanghai Cooperation Organization (SCO) with gusto, Russia has become wary of the organization, viewing it as a vehicle for Chinese ambitions. Chinese economic presence is being viewed as problematic as it tends to wipe out local industries and create few jobs because Chinese companies bring labor with them. As China pushes beyond its borders and seeks a larger role in global affairs, its wealth and clout are not only inspiring awe and respect but also generating envy and hostility.[22]

For its part, China is merely following in the footsteps of other major global powers who have asserted themselves abroad more forcefully in order to secure their interests as their economic and military capabilities increase. There is only one kind of great power, and one kind of great power tradition. China is not going to be any different. A superpower is a superpower, and it is time to shed the sophomoric naivety behind the mistaken belief that China's ascent to power will be any different; power is necessarily expansionist.

The sooner the world acknowledges this, the better it will be for global stability.

2

China in the Asia-Pacific

Changing Regional Balance of Power

It is almost conventional wisdom now that the center of gravity of global politics has shifted from Europe to the Asia-Pacific in recent years with the rise of China and India, Japan's gradual assertion of its military strength, and a significant shift in the US global force posture in favor of the Asia-Pacific. The debate now is whether the Asia-Pacific will witness rising tensions and conflicts in the coming years with various powers jockeying for influence in the region, or whether the forces of economic globalization and multilateralism will lead to peace and stability. Some have asked the question more directly: Will Europe's past be Asia's future?[1] It is, of course, difficult to answer this question now, when major powers in the Asia-Pacific such as China, India and Japan are still rising and grappling with a plethora of issues that confront any rising power in the international system. But what is clear is that all major powers are now re-evaluating their policy options vis-à-vis the region.

This chapter examines China's emerging role in the Asia-Pacific. First, the emerging balance of power in Asia-Pacific will be discussed in light of the theoretical debate on the issue, followed by a broad assessment of the role that China envisages for itself in the region. Subsequently, the evolving major power relationships in the Asia-Pacific will be analyzed.

Emerging Balance of Power in the Asia Pacific

The debate about the nature of the post-Cold War international system has been going on for more than a decade now and shows no signs of abating. Though scholars by and large accept that the US is the dominant power in the world today, there are differences with regard to how far ahead the US is relative to the other states and how long this dominance will last.

There is no consensus among scholars as to whether balancing is taking place vis-à-vis US preponderance, and if it is occurring, what form it is taking. This debate has gained additional momentum following the demonstration of US military power in Afghanistan and Iraq in recent years and the seemingly unilateral foreign policy pursued by the Bush Administration. But one reality that confronts US foreign policy is the rise of China and all that it implies for global peace and stability. Realizing that it would take decades to seriously compete with the US for global hegemony, China has focused its strategic energies on Asia. Its foreign policy is aimed at enhancing its economic and military power so that it can achieve regional hegemony in Asia. China's recent attempts to portray its rise as peaceful are merely aimed at allaying the concerns of its neighbors lest they try to counterbalance its growing influence.[2] China's readiness to negotiate with other regional states and to be an economically "responsible" power is also a signal to other states that there are greater benefits in supporting China's growing regional power rather than opposing its rise in any way. China realizes that it has thrived because it has devoted itself to economic development while letting the US police the region and the world. Even as it decries American hegemony, its leaders envision the Pax Americana extending well into the mid-twenty-first century, at least until China becomes a predominantly middle-class society and, if present trends continue, the world's largest economy.

However, while declaring that it will be focusing on internal socio-economic development for the next decade or so, China has actively pursued policies aimed at preventing the rise of other regional powers such as India and Japan, or at least to limit their development relative to itself.

While the US still remains the predominant power in the Asia-Pacific, the rise of China and India can no longer be ignored. Japan also seems ready to shed its military reticence. In many ways, while at the global level the international system remains largely unipolar, in the Asia-Pacific a multipolar regional order is gradually taking shape. According to a realist understanding of global politics, multipolar systems are inherently unstable because they generate uncertainty and make it difficult for states to draw lines between allies and adversaries, thereby often causing miscalculations.[3] Any conflict between two of the powers in the system is more likely to escalate into a general war, as the other powers will likely be tempted to join in. Minor powers are also more likely to play great powers off against each other. Power imbalances are more common in a multipolar world and tougher to predict.

A closely related realist approach to explaining war and peace, known as the power transition theory, focuses less on the number of great powers in the system and more on the shifting amount of power between those states.[4] According to one version of this theory, the largest wars result when a rising power is surpassing, or threatening to surpass, the most powerful state. While some argue that war results from the dominant power attempting to arrest the deterioration of its position, others argue that the rising power is more likely to initiate war as it seeks to gain the influence and prestige it feels it deserves because of its increased capabilities.

Whatever the case may be, all these scenarios are plausible if one looks at the Asia-Pacific today. It is a multipolar region where the US remains the predominant power. However, its primacy is increasingly being challenged by China, and this makes the region very susceptible to future instability. China's future conduct is the great regional uncertainty and at the same time the most important factor affecting regional security.

China is reshaping the strategic environment in the Asia-Pacific. China, India and Japan have long been viewed as the states with a potential for great-power status, that is, with the capacity to influence international economic, political, and military systems, but it is only in the last few years that these projections have come closer to be realized.[5] For more than a century it was Japan that dominated Asia, first as an imperial power and then as the first Asian country to achieve Western levels of economic development. It is China's turn now. China's resurgence is altering the power balance across the Asia-Pacific, and in the absence of effective regional institutions, the area is now at least as volatile as it was during the Cold War.[6]

China's growing clout was reflected in an idea bandied about during the early days of the Obama administration: namely that of a G-2, a global co-dominion of the US and China whereby China would be expected to look after and "manage" Asia-Pacific. This was enough to wake US allies in the region from their slumber. Realizing that their security concerns were being sidelined in Washington, Tokyo, Seoul, and Canberra began a concerted effort to make the new administration realize that such an arrangement would permanently marginalize the US in the strategic landscape of the region. Moreover, major players in the region started re-evaluating their own security doctrines. Even Kevin Rudd, the former Australian prime minister and a great Sinophile, was forced to come up with a security strategy for Australia that sought to hedge its bets vis-à-vis the potential threat from China and an unwillingness on the part of the US to play the role of regional balancer.

The talk then turned to a G-3 — a forum that would bring together the US, China and Japan — primarily aimed at pacifying Japan. Given the heavy US economic dependence on Beijing, a G-2 made some sense for the US, but it marginalized American allies in the region. India was perhaps the worst hit. From being viewed as a rising power and a balancer in the Asia-Pacific, India was back to being seen as a South Asian actor whose only relevance for the US was in making sure that Pakistan fought the Taliban with full vigor without getting preoccupied in Kashmir. The smaller countries of East and Southeast Asia, not to mention India's immediate neighbors who were being wooed by China, could not but note the shifting balance of power that Washington's maneuvering signaled, and they adjusted their own policies. The question that India faced was: Would countries be willing to build stronger ties with India if they saw it being marginalized by the US?

The chimera of "Chimerica," however, soon faced its inevitable demise. When the Obama Administration notified the US Congress in 2010 that it planned to sell weapon systems to Taiwan worth $6.4 billion, China's reaction was much more aggressive than it had been to similar announcements in the past. Not only was the US ambassador called in by the Chinese government to hear protests against the arms sales and warnings of serious repercussions if the deal went through, China also cancelled some of its military exchange programs with the US and announced sanctions against American companies that were supplying weapon systems to Taiwan. This announcement of sanctions came as a surprise. For the first time, China decided to penalize US companies that were engaged in commercial arms transactions and were not in violation of global non-proliferation norms.[7]

The China of today is not the China of yore. It is ready and willing to push back against the US on issues of vital national interest. It views itself as a major global player and therefore is reluctant to be viewed as a pushover any more. Beijing's traditional deference to Washington on major economic and strategic affairs is gone. Instead, there is a new assertiveness in diplomatic and military affairs. At the 2009 World Economic Forum the Chinese Premier lectured the US on how to manage its economy better. China publicly hectored White House envoy Todd Stern during the conference on climate change in Copenhagen in December 2009 and refused to give an inch to the West during the negotiations. China also forced the organizers of the 2010 World Economic Forum in Davos not to take up the issues of cyber-security and internet freedom, despite the fact that both were of interest to Western governments and businesses. To assert its growing leverage over the US, China has even signaled its interest in a substitute for the dollar in the form of International Monetary Fund (IMF) Special Drawing Rights or even gold. And senior Chinese military officers have openly demanded that their government sell some US bonds to punish Washington for its "anti-China" policies.

The West, meanwhile, is souring on China. Gone is the talk of China as a responsible stakeholder in the international system. Instead, Google's high-profile public spat with Beijing is being seen as symptomatic of the problems that China's rise continues to generate for global norms set by the West. China's undervalued remnibi is no longer a problem just for the US, and Chinese behavior is shaking the very foundations of the global trade regime. China has failed to play a constructive role in finding a solution to the North Korean and Iranian nuclear issues, much to the consternation of the West, and has in fact made it impossible for the international community to resolve these dangerous flashpoints. There is a growing fear that China might soon become the pre-eminent world power without even a superficial semblance of democracy, with grave consequences for the global order.

The rise of China is shaking up the security dynamic in the Asia-Pacific and the regional states are trying to calibrate their ties with China. This has already put the US–Japan relationship, which has been the cornerstone of East Asian security since the end of World War II, under severe strain. Bilateral disputes between Japan and the US are growing, while China has now surpassed the US as Japan's major trading partner. Meanwhile, the South-east Asian countries are becoming ever more closely intertwined with China economically and are finding it difficult to cross swords with China. Even Taiwan wants to conclude a free trade agreement with China as soon as possible. Once the China–ASEAN Free Trade

Agreement becomes operational, Taiwan's export-dependent economy will be left at a competitive disadvantage.

China is angling for regional leadership in Asia and the contest among various powers is becoming ever more interesting. Beijing is pushing for a trade pact that would include ASEAN's ten members together with China, Japan and South Korea. In an attempt to counterbalance Beijing's growing clout, Japan is proposing a broader "East Asian Community" that would add Australia, New Zealand, and India to the ASEAN+3 arrangement.

Despite the growing economic convergence between China and East Asia, China's growing diplomatic and military assertiveness is causing consternation in the region. China has hardened its position on disputed maritime boundaries with Southeast Asian countries. Beijing has started claiming that much of the South China Sea is Chinese territorial waters, defining it as a "core national interest," a phrase previously used in reference to Tibet and Taiwan. This came as a shock to regional states such as the Philippines, Malaysia, Vietnam, and Taiwan, who also have territorial claims in those waters. The South China Sea passage is too important to be controlled by a single country, particularly by one that is located far away from those waters.

When China suggests that it would like to extend its territorial waters — which according to international law usually run twelve miles from shore — to include its entire exclusive economic zone, which currently extends 200 miles from shore, it is challenging a fundamental principle of free navigation. All maritime powers have a national interest in freedom of navigation, open access to Asia's maritime commons, and respect for international law in the South China Sea.

Fears have been rising in Asia that China is seeking to use its growing maritime might to dominate not only the hydrocarbon-rich waters of the South China Sea but also its crucial shipping lanes, the lifeline of regional economies. And there were concerns in the region about America's commitment to regional security. Those concerns have been allayed by the US decision to undertake joint naval and air exercises with South Korea off the east coast of the Korean peninsula in 2010. The US also underlined its commitment to freedom of the seas in Asia by undertaking war games in the Yellow Sea despite Chinese threats. And when Beijing laid claim in 2010 to the entire South China Sea as a "core national interest" on a par with Tibet or Taiwan, the US Secretary of State, Hillary Clinton retorted by offering American support to a "collaborative diplomatic process by all claimants for resolving the various territorial disputes without coercion."[8]

This new US assertiveness vis-à-vis Beijing has been widely welcomed in the region as major power competition has been heating up in the region with the United States, Japan, and India reevaluating their strategic options vis-à-vis China.

India and China: Underlying Competition

As tensions between China and India have risen in recent months, India has been awash with predictions of China's impending attack. Most recently, it was suggested that China would attack India by 2012 primarily to divert attention from its growing domestic troubles. This suggestion received wide coverage in the Indian media, which were more interested in sensationalizing the issue than interrogating the claims with the seriousness they deserved.[9] Meanwhile, the official Chinese media picked up the story and gave it another spin. They argued that while a Chinese attack on India is highly unlikely, a conflict between the two neighbors could occur in one scenario: an aggressive Indian policy towards China on the border dispute, which would oblige China to use force. The Chinese media went on to speculate that the "China will attack India" story might just be a pretext for India's deployment of more troops in the border areas.

This curious exchange reflects an undercurrent of uneasiness that exists between the two Asian giants as they continue their ascent in the global hierarchy.[10] Even as they sign agreements with high-sounding words year after year, the distrust between the two is actually growing at an alarming rate. Economic cooperation and bilateral political as well as socio-cultural exchanges are at an all-time high. China is today India's largest trading partner. Yet this has done little to assuage each country's concerns about the other's intentions. The two sides are locked in a classic escalation of suspicion in which any action taken by one is immediately interpreted by the other as a threat to its own interests.

At the global level, the rhetoric is all about cooperation, and indeed the two sides have worked together on climate change, global trade negotiations, and to demand a restructuring of global financial institutions in view of the global economy's shifting center of gravity. At the bilateral level, however, things came to such a pass in 2009 that China took its territorial dispute with India all the way to the Asian Development Bank where it blocked an application by India for a loan that included development projects in the Indian state of Arunachal Pradesh, which China continues to claim as part of its own territory. Buoyed by the perception that the Obama Administration plans to make its ties with China the centerpiece of its foreign policy in light of growing American economic dependence on China, China has displayed a distinctly aggressive stance vis-à-vis India. The suggestion by the Chinese to the US Pacific Fleet Commander that the Indian Ocean should be recognized as a Chinese sphere of influence has raised hackles in New Delhi. China's lack of support for the US–India civilian nuclear energy cooperation pact, which it tried to block at the Nuclear Suppliers Group, together with its obstructionist stance in bringing the masterminds of the November 2008 terror attack in Mumbai to justice, has further strained ties.

Sino-Indian frictions are growing and the potential for conflict remains high. Alarm is rising in India because of frequent and strident claims being made by China regarding the Line of Actual Control in Arunachal Pradesh and Sikkim. Indians have complained that there has been a dramatic rise in Chinese intrusions into the Indian territory over the last two years, most of them along the border in regions of Arunachal Pradesh, which China refers to as "Southern Tibet." China has upped the ante on the border issue. It has been regularly protesting against the Indian Prime Minister's visit to Arunachal Pradesh for the last few years and asserting its claims over the territory, but what has caught most observers of Sino-Indian relations by surprise is the vehemence with which Beijing has contested every single recent Indian administrative and political action in the state, even denying visas to Indian citizens of Arunachal Pradesh. The Indian Foreign Minister was forced to go on record saying that the Chinese army "sometimes" does intrude into Indian territory, though he added that the issues were being addressed through established mechanisms. The recent rounds of boundary negotiations have failed, and there is a growing perception in India that China is less than willing to adhere to earlier political understandings on how to address the boundary dispute. Even the rhetoric has degenerated to an extent that a Chinese analyst connected to China's Ministry of National Defense recently claimed in an article that China could "dismember the so-called 'Indian Union' with one little move" into as many as thirty states.

India's challenge remains formidable. It has not yet achieved the economic and political power that China enjoys regionally and globally. But it gets increasingly grouped with China as a rising power, emerging power, or even future global superpower. Indian elites who have been obsessed with Pakistan for the last sixty years suddenly have found a new object of fascination. India's main security concern now is not the increasingly decrepit state of Pakistan but an ever more assertive China, which is widely viewed in India as having better strategic planning abilities. The defeat at the hands of the Chinese in 1962 has psychologically scarred the elites' perceptions of China, and they are unlikely to change in the near future. China is viewed by India as a growing, aggressive, nationalistic power whose ambitions are likely to reshape the regional and global balance of power, with deleterious consequences for Indian interests. Indian policy-makers, however, continue to believe that Beijing is not a short-term threat to India but needs to be watched over in the long term, though Indian defense officials are increasingly warning in rather blunt terms about the disparity between the two Asian powers. India has been warned by its former Naval Chief that the country neither has "the capability nor the intention to match China force for force" in military terms, while its former Air Chief has suggested that China posed more of a threat to India than Pakistan.

It may well be that the recent hardening of the Chinese posture toward India is a function of its own sense of internal vulnerabilities, but that is hardly a consolation to Indian policy-makers who have to respond to the Indian public, which increasingly wants their nation to assert itself in the region and beyond. India is rather belatedly gearing up to respond with its own diplomatic and military overtures, setting the stage for Sino-Indian strategic rivalry.

India is the country that will be and already is being most affected by a rising China. China is a rising power in both Asia and the world, and as such will do its utmost to prevent the rise of other powers around it that might challenge China's claims to regional primacy in the future. China's all-weather friendship with Pakistan; its attempts to increase its influence in Nepal, Bangladesh, and Burma; its persistent refusal to recognize parts of India such as Arunachal Pradesh; its lack of support for India's membership on the United Nations Security Council and other regional and global organizations; and its unwillingness to support the US–India nuclear pact:

all are parts of China's attempt to prevent the rise of India as a regional and global player of major importance. With India's recent rise as an economic and political power of global significance, Sino-Indian ties are now at a critical juncture, with India trying to find the right policy mix to deal with its most important neighbor.

China has always viewed India as a mere regional player and has tried to confine India to the peripheries of global politics. It was argued a few years ago that India was not on China's radar, which had set its eyes much higher. Today the rise of India poses a challenge to China in more ways than one, the most important being ideological. The success of the Indian developmental model poses a significant challenge for the Chinese regime. And India's success is being celebrated across the world, especially in the West, it is no surprise that China is becoming edgier in its relationship with India. It is notable that it was only after the US started courting India that Chinese rhetoric towards India underwent a slight modification. Realizing that a close US–India partnership would change the regional balance of power to its disadvantage, China has started tightening the screws on India. It has further entrenched itself in India's neighborhood even as Sino-Indian competition for global energy resources has increased. The development of infrastructure by China in its border regions with India has been so rapid and effective, and the Indian response so lackadaisical, that the Indian Member of Parliament from Arunachal Pradesh was forced to suggest in sheer exasperation that the government should allow Arunachal to have a rail link with China, as even sixty years after independence India has failed to connect his state to central parts of the nation.

India is now trying to catch up with China by improving the infrastructure on its side of the border areas. It has deployed two additional army divisions with heavy tanks and ramped up its air power in the region that is a bone of contention between India and China. The tensions inherent in this evolving strategic relationship were underlined in an incident when an Indian Kilo class submarine and Chinese warships, on their way to the Gulf of Aden to patrol the pirate-infested waters, reportedly engaged in maneuvers designed to test for weaknesses in each other's sonar systems. The Chinese media reported that its warships forced the Indian submarine to surface, which was strongly denied by the Indian Navy. Unless managed carefully, such incidents could easily turn serious in the future.

Both China and India are rising at the same time in an Asia-Pacific strategic landscape that is in flux. What is causing concern in Asia and beyond is the opacity that seems to surround China's military build-up, and a consensus is emerging that Beijing's real military spending is at least double the announced figure. This is because the official figures of the Chinese government do not include the cost of new weapon purchases or research. From Tokyo to New Delhi, from Jakarta to Canberra, calls are rising for China to be more open about the intentions behind its dramatic pace of military spending and its military capabilities. Whatever Chinese intentions might be, consistent increases in defense budgets over the last several years have put China on track to become a major military power, and the power most capable of challenging American dominance in the Asia-Pacific. While China's near-term focus remains on preparations for potential problems in the Taiwan Straits, its nuclear force modernization, its growing arsenal of advanced missiles, and its development of space and cyberspace technologies are changing the military balance in Asia and beyond.

A rising China will find it difficult to tolerate a rising India as its potential competitor. Even if India is a long way from challenging Chinese regional dominance, it is unlikely that China will leave anything to chance, and so will try its best to contain India, as it has already done to a large extent. And it is this containment that India will be forced to guard against. China's intentions vis-à-vis India may seem entirely peaceful at the moment, but that is largely irrelevant in the strategic scheme of things. A troubled history coupled with the structural uncertainties engendered by their simultaneous rise is propelling the two Asian giants onto paths that the two might find rather difficult to navigate in the coming years. Notwithstanding notions such as "Chindia" which have been romanticized in certain quarters, the elite consensus in India is that China should not be allowed a free hand in shaping the strategic environment of the region.

The problem, however, is that India has no real bargaining leverage vis-à-vis China, and negotiations rarely succeed in the absence of leverage. Domestic political constraints and the lack of any incentive for China to negotiate have allowed the border problem to fester for far too long. India, moreover, is not making any serious effort to get any economic, diplomatic or military leverage over its most powerful neighbor. India seems to have lost the battle over Tibet to China, despite the fact that Tibet constitutes China's only truly fundamental vulnerability vis-à-vis India. India has failed to limit China's military use of Tibet despite the major implications for Indian security, and in fact Tibet has become a platform for the projection of Chinese military power. Moreover, India has found it difficult to summon enough self-confidence to even allow peaceful protests by the Tibetans or to forcefully condemn Chinese physical assaults on its Tibetan minority and verbal assaults on the Dalai Lama.

There is nothing really sinister about China's attempts to expand its own influence and curtail India's. China is a rising power in Asia and the world, and as such will do its utmost to prevent the rise of other powers around its periphery that might in the future prevent it from taking its rightful place as a global player. It did so in 1962 when it demolished India's claims for regional leadership by defeating it in a territorial conflict, and it is doing it today. This is not much different than the stated US policy of preventing the rise of other powers that might threaten its position as a global hegemon. Just as the US is working towards achieving its strategic objective, China is pursuing its own strategic agenda.

There is also nothing extraordinarily benign in China's attempts to improve its bilateral relations with India in recent times. After cutting India down to size in various ways, China would not like to see India cooperate with the US in order to contain China. In this geopolitical chessboard, while both the US and China are using India towards their own strategic ends, India has ended up primarily reacting to the actions of the other. And the main reason for this is India's lack of recognition of the forces that drive international politics in general, coupled with its failure to come up with a coherent strategy towards China in particular.

India and China are two major powers in Asia with global aspirations and some significant conflicting interests. As a result, some amount of friction in their bilateral relationship is inevitable. If India is serious about its desire to emerge as a major global power, then it will have to tackle the challenge of China's rise. Indian foreign policy is gearing up to tackle precisely this challenge with its new approach towards the US and Japan.

India and the US: From Estrangement to Engagement

India has begun charting a new course in its foreign policy by getting closer to the US in recent years. If India is indeed a "swing state" in the international system, then it seems to have swung considerably towards the US. The demise of the Soviet Union liberated Indian and US attitudes towards each other from the structural confines of Cold War realities. As India pursued economic reforms and moved towards global integration, it was clear that the US and India will have to find a modus vivendi for a deeper engagement with each other. As Indian foreign policy priorities changed, US–India cooperation increased on a number of issues. India needed US support for its economic regeneration and the Clinton Administration viewed India as an emerging success story of globalization. Yet, the relations could only go so far in the absence of US reconciliation to India's nuclear status and the inability of the US to move beyond the India–Pakistan hyphenated relationship in South Asia.

It was the Bush Administration that redefined the parameters of US–India bilateral engagement. That India would figure prominently in Bush Administration's global strategic calculus was made clear by Condoleezza Rice in her *Foreign Affairs* article before the 2000 presidential elections in which she had argued that "there is a strong tendency to conceptually (in America) connect India with Pakistan and to think of Kashmir or the nuclear competition between the two states."[11] She made it clear that India has the potential to become a great power and US foreign policy would do well to take that into account. The Bush Administration, from the very beginning, refused to look at India through the prism of non-proliferation and had viewed India as a natural and strategic ally. It was also clear to both the US and India that the road to a healthy strategic partnership was through nuclear energy cooperation. The US–India civilian nuclear energy cooperation pact became the most potent symbol of rapprochement between the two states.

The US sees India as a close partner in enhancing security cooperation against maritime threats in the Indian Ocean area, preventing piracy, carrying out search and rescue operations, responding to natural disasters, and enhancing cooperative capabilities, including through logistical support. The Indian Navy is expected to assume a substantive role in this joint effort to ensure the security of the Indian Ocean. Since protection of the sea-lanes is of vital importance to countries such as Japan, Australia, Singapore and Indonesia, it may well become a six-nation cooperative effort. The annual Indo-US bilateral naval exercises are continuing apace with aircraft carriers from the Indian and the US navies operating together regularly. The air forces of the US and India have also conducted joint exercises in recent years which have witnessed the participation of F-16 fighters from the US and of Su-30, Mirage-2000, MiG-29, MiG-27, and Bison aircrafts from India. As part of the ongoing Indo-US defense cooperation, a South Asia Peacekeeping Operations Command Post Exercise has been undertaken for the past few years. India plays a lead role in this exercise which is attended by officers from the US, Bangladesh, Nepal, and Sri Lanka.

As a response to the rising power of China in the Pacific, the US has started adjusting its defense strategy and force posture to deal with the rising dragon in Asia. The 2006 Quadrennial Defense Review (QDR) specifically calls for boosting the number of naval ships in the Pacific Ocean. It would put six of the US Navy's twelve aircraft carriers and 60 percent of its submarine forces in the Pacific at all times to support engagement, presence, and deterrence.[12] The Pentagon is considering buying new classes of weapons suited to a twenty-first century battle in the Pacific that would feature cyber-warfare, space weapons, satellite-guided missiles, ship-borne anti-missile defenses, unmanned bombers launched from carrier decks and small, sub-hunting warships. The US is also actively expanding, diversifying and bolstering its bases in Asia so as to move them closer to China while at the same time reducing their vulnerability to attack. The US Navy has accelerated its schedule for building its next generation of cruisers by seven years and is considering buying more small anti-submarine vessels.

Theatre-range ballistic missiles, land-attack cruise missiles, anti-ship cruise missiles, surface-to-air missiles, land-based aircraft, submarines, surface combatants, amphibious ships, naval mines, nuclear weapons, and possibly high-power microwave devices have been identified by the US Congress as some of the major elements of China's military modernization that have potential implications for the future of US naval capabilities. The primary focus of China's military modernization is to be able to deploy a force that can succeed in a short-duration conflict with Taiwan and also deter US intervention or delay the arrival of US naval and air forces. But the broader agenda is to achieve Chinese dominance in Asia-Pacific and to replace the US as the regional hegemon. Today, the Chinese armed forces are already considered strong enough to delay and punish the US Navy in any confrontation over Taiwan. The US National Intelligence Council has made it clear that "China will overtake Russia and others as the second-largest defence spender after the United States over the next two decades and will be, by any measure, a first-rate military power."

The 2006 QDR makes a very strong statement of India's importance for the US in the emerging global security architecture. While a concern with China's rising military power is palpable throughout the defense review, it is instructive to note the importance that the QDR has attached to India's rising global profile. India is described as an emerging great power and a key strategic partner of the US. Shared values such as the two states being long-standing multi-ethnic democracies are underlined as providing the foundation for increased strategic cooperation. This stands in marked contrast to the unease that has been expressed with the centralization of power in Russia and lack of transparency in security affairs in China. It is also significant that India is mentioned along with America's traditional allies such as NATO countries, Japan, and Australia. The QDR goes on to say categorically that close cooperation with these partners (including India) in the war on terrorism as well in efforts to counter WMD proliferation and other non-traditional threats ensures not only the continuing need for these alliances but also for improving their capabilities.

For the US, India is now a crucial player in the emerging balance of power in the Pacific. It would like a strong US–India alliance to act as a bulwark against the arc of Islamic instability running from the Middle East to Asia and to create greater balance in Asia.[13] How India is willing to participate in this strategy will be determined by the domestic political dynamic in India.

India and Japan: Newfound Intimacy

With an eye on China, India is also increasing its ties with Japan, and India has even held joint naval exercises in the South China Sea with the US and Japan. The former Japanese Prime Minister, Shinzo Abe, underlined his desire to spread values such as freedom, democracy, human rights, and the rule of law in Asia, and India emerged as a natural partner for Japan in this endeavor. India's growing closeness to the US is also increasing Japan's inclination to take India seriously, and both countries are well aware of the Chinese strategy to contain the rise of its two most-likely challengers in the region.

Despite significant economic and trade ties between China and Japan, political tensions have increased in recent years, especially over the differing interpretations of history by the two nations.[14] There was a public outcry in China a few years back when Japan's education ministry approved history textbooks which were said to whitewash Japan's militarism in Asia during the first half of the twentieth century. The Chinese assert that about 200,000 to 300,000 Chinese were killed during the Japanese occupation of Nanjing that began in 1937, and the new Japanese textbooks refer to this merely as the "Nanjing incident." China asked Japan to take responsibility for the unrest in Chinese cities stemming from its continuing efforts to rewrite the history of its occupation of China during World War II. Unrest erupted in various Chinese cities including Beijing, Shanghai, Chengdu, and Guangzhou following the Chinese government's publication and subtle manipulation of the news about the Japanese textbooks.[15] Japan, meanwhile, asked for an apology of its own from China for the violent attacks against Japanese government offices and businesses in China. It also did not help when Tokyo's High Court rejected an appeal for compensation by Chinese survivors of biological-warfare experiments conducted by Japan during World War II. More recently, relations between China and Japan took a nosedive in September 2010 when China decided to cease high-level political exchanges with Japan to protest the extended detention of the captain of a Chinese fishing trawler captured by Japanese ships in disputed waters.[16] Beijing essentially bullied its way through the crisis and responded by not only threatening Tokyo but actually halting the exports of rare earth minerals to Japan underscoring China's growing economic leverage and its willingness to try to translate that into political power. In a classic case of coercive diplomacy, Beijing compelled Tokyo to release the Chinese fishing boat captain unconditionally. In this process, however, Beijing ended up damaging its credibility as a peaceful rising power in the Asia-Pacific and strengthened the military alliance between the US and Japan.

What is fuelling these Sino-Japanese tensions is a burgeoning sense of strategic rivalry as China's power expands across Asia and Japan redefines its regional military role in close cooperation with the United States. Japan has made it clear that it considers China a potential military threat that may have to be faced and countered in the coming years. Japan has also announced that a peaceful resolution of the Taiwan issue is a strategic objective that it shares with the United States, signaling to China that it might help America defend Taiwan in the event of a war. Against this backdrop, the burgeoning ties between India and Japan assume new significance.

India's ties with Japan have come a long way since May 1998 when a chill had set in after India's nuclear tests, with Japan imposing sanctions and suspending its Overseas Development Assistance to the country. Since then, the changing strategic environment in the Asia-Pacific has brought the two countries together, so much so that the visit of the Indian Prime Minister to Japan in 2009 resulted in the unfolding of a roadmap to transform a low-key relationship into a major strategic partnership. According to Shinzo Abe, a former Japanese Prime Minister, "the India–Japan relationship will be the most important bilateral relationship (for Japan) in the world."[17]

The rise of China is a major factor in the evolution of Indo-Japanese ties, as is the US attempt to build India into a major force capable of counterbalancing China in the region. Both India and Japan are well aware of China's not-so-subtle attempts to prevent their rise. One of the most blatant of these attempts has been China's opposition to the expansion of the United Nations Security Council to include India and Japan as permanent members. China's status as a permanent member of the Security Council and as a nuclear weapon state is something that it would be loathe to share with any other state in Asia. As India and Japan are the two nations most likely to challenge China's regional dominance, China is determined to prevent their rise. India and Japan have decided to invigorate all major aspects of their relationship ranging from investment, defense, science, and technology to civilian cooperation in space and energy security. Even on the issue of civilian nuclear cooperation, Tokyo has agreed to play a constructive approach. India's "Look East" policy of active engagement with the ASEAN and East Asia is largely predicated upon Japanese support. India's participation in the East Asia Summit was facilitated by Japan and the East Asia Community proposed by Japan to counter China's proposal of an East Asia Free Trade Area includes India. While China has resisted the inclusion of India, Australia, and New Zealand in the ASEAN, Japan has strongly backed the entry of all three nations.

It is also instructive to note that India's ties with Japan are not weighed down by any historical baggage, unlike those of most of the Japan's neighbors, who have historical disputes with Japan. As Japan moves ahead under a new generation of political leadership to emerge as a "normal" state with legitimate security interests and concomitant military capabilities, India is more than willing to lend Japan a helping hand.[18] The two nations also see a huge potential for gain from the complementarities between their economies. As the Indian economy is now galloping at an average annual growth rate of 8 percent, the Japanese economy is finally showing some signs of coming out of its two-decade-long recession. It is natural for the two states to strengthen their economic ties to build a foundation for a much broader strategic partnership.

Conclusion

China is the country whose rise is shaking up the security dynamic in the Asia-Pacific, and major powers in the region are trying to recalibrate their ties with China and with each other. For its part China has signaled to its challengers, such as Japan and India, that it will take all possible steps to prevent the emergence of other powers in its vicinity. This is not much different than the stated US policy of preventing the rise of other powers that might threaten its position as a global hegemon. In many ways, it is natural for China to view India as a potential rival for foreign capital, export markets, political influence, and aspirations for regional leadership.

Though it may be difficult for other regional powers to prevent the rise of China, they certainly would like to make it difficult for China to have unchallenged control over the region. It makes sense for India to stress cooperation while working to narrow the power disparity with China and build greater stability in Asia through strategic ties with other democracies, including the US and Japan. US and Japanese interests converge with those of India in this regard, and this dynamic will do much to shape the security architecture in the Asia-Pacific in the coming years.

3

China in South Asia
Rapidly Expanding Orbit

New Delhi has long viewed South Asia as India's exclusive sphere of influence and has sought to prevent the intervention of external powers in the affairs of the region. A policy similar to the Monroe Doctrine proclaimed for the Western Hemisphere by the United States in the nineteenth century was explored by Jawaharlal Nehru, India's first Prime Minister.[1] Since that time, the security of neighboring countries was considered to be intricately linked with India's own security. With India's rise in the global hierarchy in recent years, tensions have emerged between India's purported role on the world stage and the challenges it faces in its own neighborhood. South Asia is a difficult region and India's strategic periphery continues to witness continuous turmoil and uncertainty. The instability in Pakistan, Afghanistan, Bangladesh, Nepal, Sri Lanka, and Myanmar is a major factor preventing India from realizing its dream of becoming a major global player. This instability has stalled India's attempts at building inter-dependencies and enhancing connectivity, and the weak states around it tend to view New Delhi's hegemonic status in the region with suspicion. The conundrum India faces is that it is seen as unresponsive to the concerns of its neighbors, and any diplomatic aggressiveness on its part is viewed with suspicion and often resentment. India's position in the region makes it likely that Indian dominance will continue to be resented by its smaller neighbors, even as instability nearby continues to have the potential to upset its own delicate political balance. However, a policy of "splendid isolation" is not an option, and India's desire to emerge as a major global player will remain just that, a desire, unless it engages its immediate neighborhood more meaningfully and emerges as a net provider of regional peace and stability.

The inability of India to assume a leadership role in its neighborhood has been exploited by China, which has made a concerted attempt over the last few years to fill the void. China is today more deeply involved in South Asia than it has ever been before. This chapter examines the growing role of China in South Asia over the last decade and its implications for India. For a long time, only Pakistan among India's neighbors used China to further its strategic agenda vis-à-vis India. The China–Pakistan collusion on nuclear issues was probably the high point of this relationship. However, in recent years most of India's neighbors have made an attempt to court China as an extra-regional power in order to prevent India from asserting its regional supremacy. This strategy of using China to counterbalance India has been followed by Bangladesh, Sri Lanka, and Nepal to varying degrees. And China has only been too willing to play along, as these relationships not only enhance China's influence in South Asia but also keep India bogged down in South Asian affairs, thereby preventing its emergence from the straight-jacket of a mere "South Asia power" to a major global player, something that India has long desired.

Sino-Pakistan Ties: An All-Weather Friendship

In 1950 Pakistan was among the first countries to recognize the People's Republic of China and break diplomatic ties with the Republic of China. Based on their convergent interests vis-à-vis India, China and Pakistan reached a strategic understanding in the mid-1950s, a bond that has only become stronger over time. Sino-Pakistani ties increased in the aftermath of the 1962 Sino-Indian war when the two states signed a boundary agreement recognizing Chinese control over portions of the disputed Kashmir territory, and since then the ties have become so strong that the Chinese President Hu Jintao has described the relationship as "higher than mountains and deeper than oceans." Pakistan's President, Asif Ali Zardari, has suggested that "No relationship between two sovereign states is as unique and durable as that between Pakistan and China."[2] Maintaining close ties with China has been a priority for Islamabad, and Beijing has provided extensive economic, military, and technical assistance to Pakistan over the years. It was Pakistan that in early 1970s enabled China to cultivate its ties with the West and the US in particular, for Pakistan was the conduit for Henry Kissinger's landmark secret visit to China in 1971 and was instrumental in bringing China closer to the larger Muslim world. Pakistan enjoys a multifaceted and deep-rooted relationship with China underpinned by mutual trust and confidence. Pakistan has also supported China on all issues of importance to the latter, especially those related to the question of China's sovereignty over Taiwan, Xinjiang, and Tibet, and other sensitive issues such as human rights. China has reciprocated by supporting Pakistan's stance on Kashmir.

Over the years China has emerged as Pakistan's largest defense supplier. Military cooperation between the two countries has deepened with joint projects to produce armaments ranging from fighter jets to guided missile frigates. China is a steady source of military hardware to the resource-deficient Pakistani Army. It has not only given technological assistance to Pakistan but has also helped Pakistan to set up weapons factories. Pakistan's military modernization is dependent on Chinese largesse, with China supplying Pakistan with short-range M-11 missiles and helping Pakistan in the development of the Shaheen-1 ballistic missile.[3] In the last two decades, these two states have been actively involved in a range of joint ventures, including the JF-17 fighter aircraft used for delivering nuclear weapons, an Airborne Warning and Control System, and the Babur cruise missile (the dimensions of which exactly replicate those of the Hong Niao Chinese cruise missile). In a major move for China's indigenous defense industry, China is supplying its most advanced combat aircraft, the third-generation J-10 fighter jet, to Pakistan in a deal worth around $6 billion.[4] Beijing is helping Pakistan build and launch satellites for remote sensing and communication even as Pakistan is reportedly already hosting a Chinese space communication facility at Karachi.[5]

China has played a major role in the development of Pakistan's nuclear infrastructure and has emerged as Pakistan's benefactor at a time when increasingly stringent export controls in Western countries made it difficult for Pakistan to acquire materials and technology from other sources. The Pakistani nuclear weapons program is essentially an extension of the Chinese one. Despite being a member of the Nuclear Non-Proliferation Treaty (NPT), China has supplied Pakistan with nuclear materials and expertise and has provided critical assistance in the construction of Pakistan's nuclear facilities. As has been aptly noted by Gary Milhollin, "If you subtract China's help from Pakistan's nuclear program, there is no nuclear programme."[6] In the 1990s, China designed and supplied the heavy water Khusab reactor, which plays a key role in Pakistan's production of plutonium. A subsidiary of the China National Nuclear Corporation also contributed to Pakistan's efforts to expand its uranium enrichment capabilities by providing 5,000 custom-made ring magnets, which are an essential component of the bearings that facilitate the high-speed rotation of centrifuges. China also provided technical and material support in the completion of the Chashma Nuclear Power Reactor and plutonium reprocessing facility, which was built in the mid-1990s. Although China has long denied helping any nation attain nuclear capability, the father of Pakistan's nuclear weapons program, Abdul Qadeer Khan, has acknowledged the crucial role China has played by giving Pakistan fifty kilograms of weapons-grade enriched uranium, providing detailed plans of nuclear weapons, and tons of uranium hexafluoride for Pakistan's centrifuges.[7] This is perhaps the only case where a nuclear weapon state has passed on weapons-grade fissile material as well as a bomb design to a non-nuclear weapon state.

On the economic front, China and Pakistan have a free trade agreement with China accounting for around 11 percent of Pakistan's imports. The two sides hope to raise their annual bilateral trade to US$15 billion by 2010. China's "no-strings attached" economic aid to Pakistan is appreciated more than the aid it receives from the US, which often comes with conditions, even though Chinese assistance is nowhere near what the US gives to Pakistan. Though Beijing did provide a soft loan of about $500 million to Islamabad to help it through its economic crisis in 2008, it did not end up giving a large-scale bail-out package as was expected, and thus forced Pakistan to go to the International Monetary Fund. China's economic cooperation with Pakistan is growing, with substantial Chinese investment in Pakistani infrastructure, including the noted Pakistani deep water port in Gwadar. China is the largest investor in the Gwadar Deep-Sea Port, which is strategically located at the mouth of the Strait of Hormuz. The two states have cooperated on a variety of large-scale infrastructural projects in Pakistan, including highways, mines, electricity generation, and nuclear power projects. Over-riding Indian objections to its activities in Pakistan-Occupied Kashmir, China is busy undertaking a range of projects, the most significant being the development of a strategic transport corridor between western China and Pakistan. It is Gwadar, however, that has attracted the most attention. China's presence in the Bay of Bengal via roads and ports in Burma and in the Arabian Sea via the Chinese-built port of Gwadar has been a cause of concern for India. With access to crucial port facilities in Egypt, Iran, and Pakistan, China is well-poised to secure its interests in the region.

India has been the main factor that has influenced China's and Pakistan's policies vis-à-vis each other. Whereas Pakistan wants to gain access to civilian and military resources from China to balance Indian might in the sub-continent, China, viewing India as a potential challenger in the strategic landscape of Asia, views Pakistan as it central instrument to counter Indian power in the region. The China–Pakistan partnership serves the interests of both partners by presenting India with a potential two-front theatre in the event of war with either country.[8] Each is using the other to counterbalance India, as India's disputes with Pakistan keep India occupied and thus prevent it from attaining its potential as a major regional and global player. China meanwhile guarantees the security of Pakistan when it comes to its conflicts with India, thus preventing India from using its much superior conventional military strength against Pakistan. Not surprisingly, one of the central pillars of Pakistan's strategic policies for the last four decades or more has been its evergrowing military relationship with China. And preventing India's dominance in South Asia by strengthening Pakistan has been a strategic priority for China. As Sino-Indian ties have deteriorated in recent times, Pakistan's centrality in China's foreign policy has only increased.

The fundamental underpinnings of the Sino-Indian bilateral relationship remain highly uncertain. China has tried hard to maintain a rough balance of power in South Asia by preventing India from gaining an upper hand over Pakistan. India's preoccupation with Pakistan reduces India to the level of a regional power, while China can claim the status of an Asian and world power.[9] It is instructive to note that even though India and China have similar concerns regarding Islamic terrorism in Kashmir and Xinjiang, respectively, China has been unwilling to make a common cause with India against Pakistan. As India struggles to emerge as a global power with an ambitious foreign policy agenda, China can effectively scuttle Indian ambitions by continuing with its diplomatic and military support of Pakistan. Much to India's chagrin, China has given ample indications in the recent past that it wants to continue along that path.

With the civilian government of President Zardari under intense pressure from the United States to do more to fight terrorism emanating from Pakistani soil, there are calls in Pakistan to adopt a foreign policy which considers China and not the US to be Pakistan's strongest ally and most significant stakeholder. China's emergence as the leading global economic power, coupled with increased cooperation between India and the US, has helped this suggestion gain support. Washington has historically been accused of using Pakistan in times of need and then deserting it for a policy that favors stronger relations with India to serve its larger strategic agenda. Pakistan remains angry about the way the US used Pakistan to funnel aid to Afghan mujahideen against the Russians in Afghanistan and then turned its back on Pakistan after the Soviet withdrawal. Where only around 9 percent of Pakistanis view the US as a partner, around 80 percent of the Pakistani population considers China a friend.[10] China is considered a reliable ally which has always come to Pakistan's aid when India has seemed on the ascendant, to the extent that China has even supported Pakistan's strategy of using terror as an instrument of policy against India. Not surprisingly, Pakistan has given China a "blank check" to intervene in India–Pakistan peace talks.[11]

China has provided Pakistan most of the ordinance that its Inter-Services Intelligence (ISI) supplies to terrorist groups operating in and against India. Most of the sophisticated communications equipment used by terrorists in India, especially in Kashmir, is made in China and has been routed through the Pakistani army. The terrorists who attacked Mumbai in November 2008 used Chinese equipment. Moreover, China has continued to block UN sanctions against the dreaded Lashkar-e-Toiba (LeT) and Jamaat-ud-Dawa (JuD), the organizations that planned and executed the attacks in Mumbai, despite a broad global consensus favoring such a move.[12] It was only in December 2008 that China agreed to ban JuD as tensions surfaced between Beijing and Islamabad over the issue of Chinese Uighur separatists receiving sanctuary and training in Pakistani territory. Though counter-terror cooperation between China and Pakistan has gained traction and Pakistan has taken a number of steps to assuage the concerns of Beijing, the rise of Islamist extremism in China remains an irritant in an otherwise strong Sino-Pakistani relationship.

But with India ascending in the global hierarchy and the US continuing to build a strong partnership with India, China's need for Pakistan is likely to grow. This has been evident in Chinese polices towards Pakistan on critical issues in South Asia. As tensions rose between India and Pakistan in the aftermath of the November 2008 terror attacks in Mumbai, Pakistan's Chairman of the Joint Chiefs of Staff Committee went to China to seek support, which was readily given. The visit resulted in the signing of a new military pact between the two nations, with Beijing agreeing to expedite the delivery of F-22 frigates to Pakistan's navy. Beijing has justified its arms sales to Pakistan on the grounds that India was buying similar weapon systems from the US. Given that India has entered into similar deals for military hardware from the US and Russia, China has defended Pakistan's desire for high capacity weapons systems as normal for an independent nation seeking to bolster its security.[13]

With the exception of China, other major global powers such as Britain, France, Germany and Russia supported the US–India nuclear deal as they were eager to sell nuclear fuel, reactors and equipment to India. China, for its part, made its displeasure clear by asking India to sign the NPT and dismantle its nuclear weapons. The official Xinhua news agency of China commented that the US–India nuclear agreement "will set a bad example for other countries."[14] Since the US–India deal is in many ways a recognition of India's rising global profile, China, not surprisingly, was not very happy with the outcome and indicated that it would be willing to sell nuclear reactors to Pakistan.[15] It was a not-so-subtle message to the US that if Washington decides to play favorites, China also retains the same right. China's plans to supply two nuclear reactors to Pakistan in defiance of international rules have gathered momentum. Chinese authorities have confirmed that the China National Nuclear Corporation has signed an agreement with Pakistan for two new nuclear reactors at the Chashma site — Chashma III and Chashma IV — in addition to the two that it is already working on in Pakistan. This action of China will be in clear violation of the Nuclear Suppliers Group (NSG) guidelines which forbid nuclear transfers to countries that are not signatories to the NPT and/or do not adhere to comprehensive international safeguards on their nuclear programs. China has suggested that "there are compelling political reasons concerning the stability of South Asia to justify the exports," echoing Pakistan's oft-repeated compliant that the US–India nuclear pact has upset stability in the region by assisting India's strategic program.[16] The decision to supply reactors to Pakistan, a non-signatory to the NPT with a record of dealing with North Korea, Iran and Libya, reflects China's growing diplomatic confidence and underscores its view of Pakistan as a strategic South Asian power.

Beginning in 1962, Chinese strategists decided that they can deal with India on their own terms. But with the US entering the equation, all kinds of uncertainties have been introduced into Chinese planning. China's involvement in the construction of Gwadar has worried India due to the port's strategic location, about 70 kilometers from the Iranian border and 400 kilometers east of the Strait of Hormuz, a major oil supply route. It has been suggested that Gwadar will provide China with a "listening post" from which it can "monitor US naval activity in the Persian Gulf, Indian activity in the Arabian Sea, and future US–Indian maritime cooperation in the Indian Ocean."[17] Though Pakistan's naval capabilities do not, on their own, pose any challenge to India, the combination of Chinese and Pakistani naval forces can indeed be difficult for India to counter. Recent suggestions emanating from Beijing that China is likely to set up military bases overseas to counter American influence and exert pressure on India have been interpreted in certain sections in New Delhi as a veiled reference to China's interest in having a permanent military presence in Pakistan. Even though it might not be politically possible for the Pakistani government to openly allow China to set up a military base, New Delhi fears that Islamabad might allow Beijing use of its military facilities without any public announcements about it.[18] India's 2008–09 annual defense report registers concerns regarding Chinese-Pakistani collusion by underlining China's "assistance and cooperation with Pakistan" as well as "the possibility of enhancing connectivity with Pakistan through the territory of Jammu and Kashmir illegally occupied by China and Pakistan."[19]

It has been suggested that the rapidly deteriorating situation in Pakistan and its long-term consequences for regional stability might result in greater cooperation between Beijing and New Delhi aimed at stabilizing the shared periphery between the two nations. The turbulence in Xinjiang has forced Beijing to pay greater attention to the sources of international terrorism in Pakistan, with the prospect of Islamist extremism spilling over from Afghanistan and Pakistan into the restive Xinjiang province, which saw clashes between Han Chinese and the Muslim Uighurs in 2009. Yet concerns have increased in India in recent times that China and Pakistan are coordinating their efforts on the border issue against India, with China's positioning on the Line of Actual Control (LAC) becoming more aggressive than ever.[20]

Historically, China has supported Pakistan and other smaller states in South Asia to oppose what it viewed as India's hegemonic ambitions in the region. Now as India seeks to become a major global power, support for Pakistan assumes an even greater significance as Pakistan alone among South Asian states has the ability to constrain India to an extent that would help Beijing strategically. China has used its special relationship with Pakistan to pursue classic balance of power politics vis-à-vis India. This policy has been rather successful in so far as India has found it difficult to emerge out of the straightjacket of being a South Asian power, despite its long-standing perception of itself as a major global power. As recently as 2009, the US President could go to Beijing and acknowledge that China has a role to play in the India–Pakistan relationship.[21] It has been correctly noted that China's policy towards Pakistan is "an object lesson in how to attain long-term national goals by calm calculation, forbearance, and diplomatic skill."[22]

A rising India makes Pakistan all the more important to China's strategy for the subcontinent. It is highly unlikely that China will give up playing the Pakistan card vis-à-vis India anytime soon.

China and Bangladesh: Following the Sino-Pak Trajectory

Bangladesh is surrounded on three sides by India along a 4,094-kilometer-long border. This results in the country's almost total geographical domination by India except for the 193-kilometer-long border that Bangladesh shares with Myanmar. India's power in South Asia, in fact, has been a cause for concern for all of its smaller neighbors. Bangladesh is no exception. For India, the struggle against Pakistan in 1971 was a strategic imperative; India further marginalized Pakistan by cutting it in half to create Bangladesh. India may have expected Bangladesh to remain indebted to it for its assistance in giving Bangladesh its independence, but this did not happen. After all, structural constraints are the most important determinant of state behavior in international politics, and Bangladesh soon began "balancing" against Indian preponderance in the region. Like other states in South Asia, Bangladesh has tried to counter India's regional hegemony through a variety of means.

Bangladesh's relations with Pakistan in the years immediately after independence were severely strained for obvious reasons, but their ties eventually began to improve quite dramatically. A major impetus for this was the desire of both countries to balance India's power and influence in the region. In 1974 Pakistan and Bangladesh signed an accord to recognize each other, and two years later established formal diplomatic relations. The two states have maintained high-level contacts ever since. It has been correctly observed that popular fears of Indian domination in both countries outweigh any lingering animosity between them, resulting in closer Pakistan–Bangladesh ties.[23] Thus Bangladesh started cultivating Pakistan in an effort to counterbalance India because it started viewing India as its main potential threat. In contrast, India's foreign policy obsession with Pakistan has led it to ignore Bangladesh. The former Pakistani President General Pervez Musharraf reportedly used his 2003 visit to Bangladesh to forge covert military ties with Dhaka and obtain authorization for Pakistan's premier intelligence agency, Inter-Services Intelligence (ISI), to operate from Bangladeshi territory. Growing closeness to Pakistan has enabled Bangladesh to establish links with China, Pakistan's closest ally in the region.

Bangladesh has made a systematic attempt in recent years to woo an extra-regional power — namely China — in order to prevent New Delhi from asserting regional supremacy in its relations with Dhaka. This strategy is not typical of Bangladesh's foreign policy, but other states in the region — including Pakistan, Sri Lanka, and Nepal — have also used China to try to counterbalance India. Bangladesh has been more than willing to play off Pakistan and China against India. China for its part has made a serious effort in recent years to wean Bangladesh away from India's influence, thereby further enhancing its own role in South Asia.

Since China and Bangladesh established ties in 1976 their bilateral relationship has grown steadily, culminating in the signing of a "Defense Cooperation Agreement" in 2002 that covers military training and weapons production. It was aimed at bolstering Bangladesh's defense forces: the armed forces of Bangladesh, like those of Pakistan, are predominantly equipped with Chinese military hardware. This agreement was the first of its type ever signed by Bangladesh in its history. It was a period when Bangladesh was under pressure from India for allowing its territory to be used for anti-Indian activities. Bangladesh might have felt the need to engage

China more substantively to signal to India that it would not tolerate too much pressure the issue. Dhaka has emerged as the prime buyer of weapons made in China, including 122-mm Howitzers, rocket launchers, small arms like pistols and sub-machine guns, and regular 82-mm mortars.[24] Bangladesh's missile launch pad near the Chittagong Port was also constructed with assistance from China. It successfully test fired land-based anti-ship cruise missile C-802A, a modified version of the Chinese Ying Ji-802, with a strike range of 120 km, in 2008 with the active participation of Chinese experts.[25]

China has also provided Bangladesh with substantial resources to bolster its civil service and law enforcement agencies. The two states have signed an agreement on peaceful uses of nuclear energy in the fields of medicine, agriculture, and biotechnology.[26] China is now Bangladesh's largest source of imports and Bangladesh is the third-largest trade partner of China in South Asia. Bilateral trade has increased from $1.1 billion in 2002 to $4 billion in 2008, and crossing $5.5 billion in 2010. There is growing Chinese investment in a range of sectors in Bangladesh, especially in small and medium-sized enterprises. China is investing in important infrastructure development projects and is providing duty-free access to Bangladeshi products in its markets. Energy-hungry China views Bangladesh's large natural gas reserves as a potential asset to be tapped and, much to India's dismay, Bangladesh supports China's entry into the South Asian Association for Regional Cooperation (SAARC). It was at the invitation of Bangladesh that China was given an observer status in the SAARC. China has offered to assist in the construction of nuclear power plants in Bangladesh to help meet the country's growing energy needs even as it is making a push towards the development of natural gas reserves of Bangladesh. While Bangladesh has granted China exploration rights for developing its natural gas fields, friction between India and Bangladesh has precluded cooperation between India and Bangladesh on the issue of energy. Energy cooperation between China and Bangladesh is growing: Chinese oil companies are helping to develop oil and gas reserves in Bangladesh, with the potential of Bangladesh exporting oil to China. There is a desire in Dhaka to construct an oil pipeline from Chittagong to Kunming in China. China is also helping Bangladesh in the construction of a deep water port at Chittagong and is investing in the deep sea port at Sonadia, heightening Indian fears of "encirclement."

In this context, it is interesting to note the proposal to revive the

Stilwell Road (also known as the "Old Burma Road") which stretches from the Indian state of Assam through Bangladesh and Myanmar all the way to Yunnan Province in southern China. In 1999 China, India, Myanmar, and Bangladesh all came together in what is known as the "Kunming Initiative" to push this proposal forward, mainly because of the potential trade advantages that would derive from linking those countries to Southeast Asia via a long land route.[27] But India has been reconsidering this proposal, fearing that it might give a fillip to insurgents in north-eastern India who receive support from Bangladesh, and that it would also allow Chinese goods to flood Indian markets. Bangladesh has offered transit rights to China as it seeks to establish road and rail links between Chittagong and Kunming through Myanmar, something India is not very comfortable with. After agreeing to allow New Delhi to use Chittagong and Mangla port facilities, Bangladesh has offered the same to Beijing. Dhaka has also sought Chinese assistance for its proposed deep sea port in the Bay of Bengal.[28] China is funding the development of Bangladesh's Chittagong port and also the construction of a highway linking Kunming, in southwestern Yunnan province, to Chittagong via Myanmar, to give China the ability to make use of the port.

By courting Bangladesh, China will be able to get a strategic toe-hold in India's eastern flank. The development of the Chittagong port, much like the development of Gwadar in Pakistan, is aimed at facilitating China's entry into the Bay of Bengal. Though the Chittagong port is apparently being developed for commercial purposes, it could easily be used for staging Chinese naval assets. China's access to the port will bring it closer to Myanmar's oil fields. Close Sino-Bangladesh relations also further enhance Indian vulnerabilities in the critical north-eastern region. There are growing fears in India that Indian security would be gravely damaged if Dhaka decides to grant military basing rights to China. A close strategic relationship with Bangladesh will allow China to link its electronic listening systems on Coco Island in Myanmar with the staging systems in Bangladesh to monitor Indian naval and missile activities, even as the prospect of Chinese ships operating in the Andaman Sea would seriously constrain Indian power projection.[29]

While Sino-Bangladeshi ties have burgeoned under non-Awami League political dispensations in Dhaka, even the Awami League has been careful in courting China, avoiding the appearance of being under Indian influence. The military cooperation between the two has continued to gather momentum regardless of who is in power in Dhaka. A close relationship with China is one of the most potent ways in which Dhaka can demonstrate its autonomy from India.[30] Sheikh Hasina has described China as the "most dependable and consistent friend of Bangladesh" ever since the two states established their diplomatic ties more than three decades ago.[31] Given the growing closeness between China and Bangladesh, it is not surprising that the term "all weather friendship" — usually reserved to describe China's ties with Pakistan — is now also being used to describe the Sino-Bangladeshi bilateral relationship.[32]

China in Sri Lanka: The Liberation Tigers of Tamil Eelam (LTTE) and After

If New Delhi has consistently sought to exclude a hostile third-party presence from Sri Lanka, growing Chinese presence in the country poses a serious challenge to Indian policy.[33] Colombo's centrality between Aden and Singapore makes it extremely significant strategically for Indian power projection possibilities. After initially following India's lead in international affairs, even demanding that the British leave their naval base at Trincomalee and air base at Katunayake in 1957, Colombo gradually gravitated towards a more independent foreign policy. After the Chinese victory in its 1962 war with India, Colombo started courting Beijing much more seriously. Beijing, for its part, viewed New Delhi's role in Sri Lankan affairs as a means not only to "control" Sri Lanka and achieve "regional hegemony" in South Asia but also to "expel the influence of other countries."[34] The Indo-Sri Lankan agreement of 1987, whereby the two sides agreed that neither would allow its territory to be used against the security interests of other, and Colombo guaranteed that foreign military and intelligence personnel in Sri Lanka would not hurt Indo-Sri Lankan ties, merely confirmed Beijing's suspicions that India wishes to exert control over affairs in Sri Lanka.[35] Sri Lanka's support of China on the question of China's sovereignty over Taiwan and Tibet, and China's support for issues related to Sri Lankan territorial integrity, have reinforced the Sino-Sri Lankan bilateral relationship. But given Beijing's inability to effectively project power in South Asia till the early 1990s, it could only be a marginal player in the Indo-Sri Lankan dynamic and was forced to accept India's central role in Sri Lanka, especially as India seemed willing to pursue coercive diplomacy till the late 1980s.

With the Sri Lankan military declaring victory over the Liberation Tigers of Tamil Eelam (LTTE) in 2009, New Delhi has been forced to dramatically recalibrate its strategy toward the island nation and has been desperately seeking a voice in the rapidly evolving situation in Sri Lanka.[36] Colombo has promised to undertake major development projects in former Tiger-controlled areas in the north and has pledged to protect the rights of the minority Tamils. But the death of Tamil leader Velupillai Prabhakaran in 2009 sparked incidents of violence across the Indian state of Tamil Nadu, underlining the balancing act that New Delhi must perform. When the Mahinda Rajapaksa regime decided in 2007 that the time for a steady military offensive against the LTTE had come, not only was the LTTE bereft of significant outside support, but the Sri Lankan government was assured of Chinese support.[37]

China and Pakistan emerged as the main arms suppliers to Sri Lanka because India, due to the sensitivities of its Tamil population, was only able to supply arms to Colombo for defensive purposes. Colombo has astutely cultivated ties with both China and Pakistan over the last several years to keep India in check. Like most of India's neighbors, Colombo tried to balance India's regional dominance by courting extra-regional powers. China has emerged as a major player in this context, giving Sri Lanka greater strategic room to maneuver. For China, its ties with Colombo give it a foothold near crucial sea-lanes in the Indian Ocean as well as entry into what India considers its sphere of influence. China not only supplies military hardware and training, but also helps Colombo in gas exploration and in building a modern port in Hambantota. China's arms transfers include fighter aircraft, armored personnel carriers, anti-aircraft guns, air surveillance radar, rocket-propelled grenade launchers, and missiles, strengthening the position of the Sri Lankan Army against the first terrorist organization to boast an army, navy and air force along with a small submarine force. Sri Lanka's victory over the LTTE would not have been possible without the support it received from China. In the beginning China only provided political and diplomatic support to Sri Lanka in its fight against the Tigers, and Colombo was reluctant to seek Beijing's help for fear of antagonizing India. But when Rajapaksa, after being humiliated with the discovery of

LTTE air prowess, decided to launch an all-out offensive against the Tamil rebels, he decided to court China more actively in the defense sphere.

When India made it clear that it could not send offensive weapons and weapon systems such as radar, and the West decided to suspend military aid because of human rights concerns, China came to the rescue of the Sri Lankan government. Sri Lanka signed a $37.6 million deal in 2007 to buy Chinese ammunition and ordnance for its army and navy even as China supplied Sri Lanka fighter jets to counter the LTTE's air prowess. Chinese military supplies to Sri Lanka are currently estimated at $100 million per annum, with China helping Sri Lankan defense forces improve its capabilities for high-tech aerial warfare, and also generally restructure and reorient themselves. China has encouraged the Sri Lankan military's participation in multilateral regional military activities and Sri Lanka was accepted as a Dialogue Partner to the Shanghai Cooperation Organization (SCO) in 2009.

China has also displaced Japan as Sri Lanka's major aid donor, supplying the country with an annual aid package of $1 billion. Bilateral trade between China and Sri Lanka has doubled over the last five years, and China has emerged as Sri Lanka's largest trading partner. Chinese investment in infrastructure and oil exploration projects in Sri Lanka has also gathered momentum. China is providing interest-free loans and preferential loans at subsidized rates to Sri Lanka for the development of its infrastructure. It is the first foreign country to have an exclusive economic zone in Sri Lanka. China is involved in a range of infrastructure development projects in Sri Lanka: constructing power plants, modernizing Sri Lankan railways, and providing financial and technical assistance in the launching of communication satellites. China is financing more than 85 percent of the Hambantota Development Zone which will be completed over the next decade. This will include an international container port, a bunkering system, an oil refinery, and an international airport and other facilities. The port in Hambantota, deeper than the one at Colombo, is to be used as a refueling and docking station for the Chinese navy.[38] Though both nations claim that this is merely a commercial venture, its future use as a strategic asset by China remains a real possibility, much to India's consternation. For China, Hambantota will not only be an important transit point for general cargo and oil, but a presence in Hambantota also enhances

China's monitoring and intelligence gathering capabilities vis-à-vis India.

India's political and economic influence in Sri Lanka is gradually shrinking as Colombo's courting of China gives it greater room for diplomatic maneuvering vis-à-vis New Delhi. It was India's hands-off policy towards Sri Lanka, stemming from strong domestic Tamil sentiment against supporting Sri Lankan counter-insurgency efforts, which allowed China to move in. As the Tamil Tigers came close to defeating the Sri Lankan forces, the island nation asked India for assistance, but all India could do was offer financial assistance, even as Colombo turned first to Islamabad and then to Beijing for military supplies. In so doing, India gave the Rajapaksa regime a free hand to defeat the LTTE, and with this India's strategic space in Sri Lanka shrank to an all-time low despite its geo-strategic advantage and economic clout.[39] Beijing's diplomatic support helped Colombo deflect western criticism of its human rights record in defeating the LTTE.

India has expressed its displeasure about growing Chinese involvement in Sri Lanka on a number of occasions. In 2007, India's National Security Advisor openly criticized Sri Lanka for attempting to purchase a Chinese-built radar system on the grounds that it would "overreach" into Indian air space.[40] India has meanwhile failed to exert its leverage over the humanitarian troubles faced by the Tamils trapped in the fighting. New Delhi's attempts to end the war and avert humanitarian tragedy in north-east Sri Lanka proved utterly futile.

Sri Lanka has emerged stronger and more stable after its military success in the Eelam War and two national elections. To counter Chinese influence, India has been forced to step up its diplomatic offensive and offer Colombo reconstruction aid. With the LTTE now out of the picture, the Indian government is hoping that it will have greater strategic space to manage bilateral ties. However, while New Delhi will have to continue to balance its domestic sensitivities and strategic interests, Beijing faces no such constraint in developing even stronger ties with Colombo. As a consequence, India is struggling to make itself more relevant to Sri Lanka than China.

China and Nepal: Growing Reach in the Era of the Maoists

Despite being a tiny landlocked state, Nepal has a pivotal position in the South Asian geo-strategic environment as it shares a border of 1236 kilometers with China and 1690 kilometers with India.[41] For both China and India, therefore, Nepal holds great strategic value. "A yam between two rocks" was how the founder of Nepal, Prithvi Narayan Shah, described the kingdom. For China, Nepal's strategic significance lies, first and foremost, in its close proximity to Tibet. Nepal, according to Beijing, constitutes a vital part of an inner security ring that cannot be allowed to be breached by any global or regional power.[42] The Chinese occupation of Tibet in 1950 significantly increased Nepal's strategic importance for China. Ensuring Nepal's neutrality on the issue of Tibet, and securing active Nepali cooperation to prevent Tibetans from launching anti-China activities, was Beijing's primary objective in Nepal. For China, the growing influence of India had grave implications for its security considerations, especially as regards Tibet. Thus, preserving a favorable balance of power in southern Asia became the principal strategic objective of Beijing's Nepal policy. Securing Nepal's active cooperation to prevent its rivals' use of the country for anti-China activities became the primary Chinese strategic objective in Nepal.[43]

For India, Nepal remains the principal strategic land barrier between China and its own resource rich-Gangetic Plain. India's strategic stakes in Nepal dramatically increased with the Communist victory in China and the country's subsequent occupation of Tibet in 1950. Since the middle of the nineteenth century, Tibet, rather than Nepal, had served as India's buffer with China. The role of buffer passed on to Nepal after the Chinese annexation of Tibet. It became imperative for New Delhi to deny China direct access to Nepal because of the vulnerability of India's Gangetic Plain, which contains critical human and economic resources.[44]

Nepal's strategic importance has led Beijing to focus its policies on preserving and enhancing the Himalayan state's independence and neutrality by trying to reduce its dependence on India in the political, economic, and security arenas. China's policy options, however have been severely circumscribed by the special security relationship between India and Nepal formalized in the 1950 Peace and Friendship Treaty between the two.[45] In the early years of the

Cold War, Beijing, wary of an alliance between the United States and India, accepted India's preeminent position in Nepal, and followed India's lead in its relations with Nepal. Diplomatic links between China and Nepal were established only in August 1955. China, in deference to India, agreed to handle its relations with Nepal through its embassy in New Delhi. Nonetheless, Beijing continued to engage Nepal by providing economic aid and by strongly supporting Kathmandu in its disputes with New Delhi on issues of trade and transit, thereby increasing its influence among Nepalese elites.

As China's economic and political power increased, it became more assertive in Nepal. By the late 1980s, China's engagement with Nepal had grown substantially. It signed a secret intelligence sharing agreement with Nepal in 1988 and agreed to supply arms. This arms agreement elicited a strong reaction from India which imposed an economic blockade on Nepal from 1989 to 1990.[46] This did not prevent economic interactions between China and Nepal from gathering momentum in the next decade. Despite its 1950 treaty with India, Nepal began importing Chinese weaponry and sought extensive military cooperation with China in a move to reduce its dependence on India. When the US, the UK, and India refused to supply arms to the regime of King Gyanendra, China responded by dispatching arms to Nepal despite the king's anti-Maoist ideological stance. China supported the Nepalese King Gyanendra's anti-democratic measures in the name of political stability, but was nimble enough to shift its support to the Maoists as they gained ascendancy in Nepalese politics. China became the first country to provide military assistance to the Maoist government.

Over the years, China's policy towards Nepal has been guided by its larger strategic game plan vis-à-vis South Asia. In the initial years of the Cold War when Beijing was worried about a possible alliance between India and the United States, it treated Nepal cautiously so as not to offend India. However, once China gained confidence and international respect, it went all out to increase its influence in Nepal. By supporting Kathmandu's position during most disputes between India and Nepal, Beijing was able to project itself as a benevolent power, in contrast with supercilious attitude of India towards its smaller neighbors. It was also able to upgrade its military ties with Nepal, despite India's stiff resistance. As ethnic tensions have risen in Tibet in recent times, China has sought to curb the activities of Tibetan refugees in Nepal. China's interest and presence in Nepal, however, has gradually expanded and now goes far beyond the Tibet Issue. China is projecting its "soft power" in Nepal by setting up China Study Centers (CSCs) that are being used to promote Chinese values among the Nepalese populace, which is otherwise tied culturally to India. These centers are emerging as effective instruments in promoting Chinese perspectives on key issues concerning Nepal. China is constructing a 770-kilometre railway line to connect the Tibetan capital of Lhasa with the Nepalese town of Khasa, a move that will connect Nepal to China's national rail network. China is also constructing a 17-kilometere long road through the Himalayas linking Tibet to the Nepalese town of Syabrunesi which will not only connect Tibet to Nepal, but when completed will also establish the first direct Chinese land route to New Delhi. China views Nepal as a vital bridge toward South Asia. China has increased its aid to Nepal substantially in the last few years and the trade volume between the two is growing, though the trade balance continues to remain heavily in favor of China, something that China is trying to address by providing duty-free access to Nepali goods in China. China's strategy of providing aid without any conditions and support for building infrastructure is enhancing China's role even as Chinese products are flooding the Nepalese market and replacing Indian ones. By painting India as a creator of instability and an undue beneficiary of Nepal's resources, China has used Nepalese sensitivities vis-à-vis Indian influence to good effect, thereby further undercutting Indian influence in Kathmandu. India's overwhelming presence remains a source of resentment towards India in Nepal. China appears attractive because it can claim that unlike India it is not interested in the internal affairs of Nepal.

The success of a democratic Nepal at peace with its neighbors is essential for the entire region, but what is of far greater importance for India is the trajectory of Nepal's foreign policy. India was concerned that the rise of the Maoists in Nepal could marginalize India in the Himalayan kingdom's foreign affairs. The Maoist-led government indeed made a decisive shift towards Beijing when it suggested that Nepal would maintain equidistance from both China and India.[47] The Maoist leader Prachanda, after becoming prime minister, broke the long-standing tradition of Nepalese heads of state of making their first foreign trip to India, and decided make China his first destination, ostensibly to attend the opening ceremonies of the 2008 Olympic Games in Beijing. China also pushed the Maoist government to sign a new treaty to replace the 1960 Peace and Friendship Treaty between China and Nepal. The Maoist government made clear its intention to re-negotiate the 1950 treaty with India, but before they could accomplish that objective, the government fell.

While it was the fear of the unknown that haunted India after the victory of the Maoists, it was clear that other political entities in Nepal, the monarchy in particular, had not been particularly well-disposed towards India for the last several years. Nepal under the Maoist regime has been no different than Nepal under its discredited monarch, who did his best to play off China against India to increase his time in power. Recent events in Nepal — culminating in the resignation of Maoist Prime Minister Prachanda and the possibility of resumption of conflict between the Maoists and the military — have again created problems for India. Maoists have spoken of their being a "foreign hand" behind recent events, and few Nepalese take this as anything but an allusion to India. The resignation of the Maoist-led government in Nepal has plunged the Himalayan kingdom into crisis and India is being blamed for pulling strings behind the scenes. New Delhi must allay concerns that it is interested in controlling Nepalese politics while quietly nudging Nepalese political parties into forming a stable government and working to counter China's growing influence. As Tibet develops economically and transport links emerge between Nepal and China, China's ability to project power in Nepal is likely to increase even further.

Conclusion

India's growing willingness to look beyond the confines of South Asia is also shaping the current trajectory of its foreign and security policy. India was long viewed by the world through the prism of its conflict with Pakistan. As India has emerged as an economic powerhouse supported by its democratic institutions, its strategic weight in global politics has grown to the point where it is viewed as one of the six members of the global balance of power configuration, alongside the United States, China, the EU, Japan, and Russia. Indian foreign policy, as a result, is more ambitious in its scope today than it has ever been, as is evident from India's engagements with states in Africa, Latin America, and the Middle East as well as with the traditional power centers. Yet it is in India's own neighborhood that India seems to be rapidly losing ground to China. India's long-term challenge in South Asia is about the impact of a rising China on the politics of the subcontinent.

China's strategy towards South Asia is premised on encircling India and confining her ambitions and influence within the region. China has started building a number of roads and ports in the states neighboring India's and is deepening its military and economic engagements with those countries, allowing it to envision a larger role for itself in the region. China began its strategy of containing India within South Asia through the use of its proxies with Pakistan and has gradually involved other states in the region, including Bangladesh, Sri Lanka, and Nepal. China is investing in several modern ports around India that can be used for strategic purposes. It is entering markets in South Asia more aggressively through both trade and investment by improving its relations with South Asian states through treaties and bilateral cooperation. China's actions have signaled to India that even as India tries to become something larger than a South Asian power by forging a strategic partnership with the US, China will do its utmost to contain India by building up its neighboring adversaries.

Not surprisingly, China's quiet maneuvers in India's backyard have allowed various smaller countries to play China off against India. In South Asia, most states are now using the China card to balance the dominance of India. This is a standard strategy adopted by small states in regional systems that are dominated by two or more major powers.[48] Small states seek to preserve their sovereignty by resorting to strategies that seek to balance great powers locked in competition for regional hegemony. These small states promote their national interests by not explicitly aligning with any one major power, but pursue policies that preserve their independent existence. Such is the case with the states in South Asia too. Forced to exist between their two giant neighbors, the smaller states in South Asia have responded by balancing those neighbors against each other.

As India's power has increased over the last two decades, it has become more confident in its rising status and has pursued a more proactive foreign policy, moving away from the idealism of the past to greater "strategic realism." This has allowed New Delhi to more vigorously pursue its interests globally and challenge China's rising dominance in the Asia-Pacific and the Indian Ocean region in particular. As a consequence, not only have Sino-Indian relations become overtly hostile, but the centrality of South Asia in China's foreign policy has also become more and more clear.

India's structural dominance in South Asia makes it a natural target of resentment among its smaller neighbors, and therefore most of these states have sought to balance Indian influence by courting China. India's challenge is twofold. First, it must engage its neighbors in a productive manner that will allow it to realize its dream of emerging as a global power. Second, it must prevent China from gaining a strategic foothold in South Asia and preserve its influence in the region. India's interests in nudging its neighbors towards political moderation, economic modernization, and regional integration are in tune with those of the broader international community. Yet for all the talk of India as a rising global power, the country has found it difficult to emerge as a leader in its own backyard. New Delhi does not seem to have a clear regional policy and by not being proactive, it has ceded the strategic space to other actors, the most significant of which is China. China's presence looms large over the subcontinent, and China has emerged as the single most important external power influencing the region. China's growing reach in South Asia has weakened New Delhi's influence, alarming Indian policymakers. These actions are in keeping with China's long-standing policy of preventing India from joining the ranks of major global powers and of confining its influence to South Asia.[49] It is to be expected that China will try to prevent India's rise by using Pakistan as a countervailing force and by cultivating India's neighbors so that New Delhi cannot emerge as the unchallenged hegemon in South Asia. This strategy seems to be working at the moment, for India finds itself politically isolated in its region. In fact it remains far from clear whether India has yet found a way of asserting its power and at the same time of containing China's rapidly increasing influence in the region.

4

China in the Indian Ocean
Challenging India's Geographical Predominance

The Indian Ocean has long been the hub of great power rivalry, and the struggle for its domination has been a perennial feature of global politics. It is third largest of the world's five oceans and straddles Asia in the north, Africa in the west, Indochina in the east, and Antarctica in the south. Home to four critical access waterways — the Suez Canal, Bab-el Mandeb (the Mandab Strait), the Strait of Hormuz, and the Strait of Malacca — the Indian Ocean connects the Middle East, Africa and East Asia with Europe and the Americas.[1] Given its crucial geographical role, major powers have long vied with each other for its control, though it was only in the nineteenth century that Great Britain was able to achieve an over-whelming dominance in the region. With the decline in Britain's relative power and the emergence of two superpowers during the Cold War, the Indian Ocean region became another arena where the US and the former Soviet Union struggled to expand their power and influence. The US, however, has remained the most significant player in the region for the last several years.

Given the rise of major economic powers in the Asia-Pacific that rely on energy imports to sustain their economic growth, the Indian Ocean region has assumed a new importance as various powers are once again vying for control of the waves in this part of the world. Nearly half of the world's seaborne trade passes across the Indian Ocean and approximately 20 percent of this trade consists of energy resources. It has also been estimated that around 40 percent of the world's offshore oil production comes from the Indian Ocean, while 65 percent of the world's oil and 35 percent of its gas reserves are found in the littoral states of this ocean.[2] Unlike the trade on the Pacific and Atlantic Oceans, almost three-quarters of trade traversing the Indian Ocean, primarily oil and gas, belongs to states external to the region. The free and uninterrupted flow of oil and goods through the ocean's Sea Lanes of Communication (SLOCs) is deemed vital for the global economy, and so all major states have a stake in a stable Indian Ocean region. It is for this reason that during the Cold War years when US–Soviet rivalry was at its height, the states bordering the Indian Ocean sought to declare the region a "zone of peace" to allow for free trade and commerce across the sea lanes of the Indian Ocean. Today, the reliance is on the US for the provision of a collective good: a stable Indian Ocean region.

This chapter explores the China's increasing influence in the Indian Ocean in the context of China's rise as a major regional and global actor. It argues that although India has historically viewed the Indian Ocean region as one in which it would like to establish its dominance, its limited material capabilities have constrained its options. With the expansion of India's economic and military capabilities, Indian ambitions in this region are soaring once again, but China's growing power in the Indian Ocean is posing a serious challenges to India. China has a significant stake in the region today, and preponderance in the Indian Ocean region, though much desired by the Indian strategic elites, remains an unrealistic aspiration for India.

China's Foray in the Indian Ocean

China emerged as the biggest military spender in the Asia-Pacific in 2006, overtaking Japan, and now has the fourth-largest defense budget in the world. The exact details of Chinese military expenditures remain contested, with estimates ranging from the official Chinese figure of $35 billion to the US Defense Intelligence Agency's estimate of $80–115 billion.[3] But the rapid rise in Chinese military expenditure is clear, with an increase of 195 percent over the decade 1997–2006. The official figures of the Chinese government do not include the cost of new weapon purchases, research or other big-ticket items. From Washington to Tokyo, from Brussels to Canberra, calls are rising for China to be more open about the intentions behind this dramatic pace of spending increase and the scope of its military capabilities. The Chinese Navy, according to a Chinese Defense white paper of 2006, will be aiming at a "gradual extension of the strategic depth for offshore defensive operations and enhancing its capabilities in integrated maritime operations and nuclear counter-attacks."[4]

China's navy is now considered the third-largest in the world behind only the US and Russia, and superior to the Indian Navy in both qualitative and quantitative terms.[5] The Peoples' Liberation Army (PLA) Navy has traditionally been a coastal force and China has had a continental outlook to security. But with the increase in its economic might since the 1980s, Chinese interests have expanded and the country has acquired a maritime orientation with the intention of projecting power into the Indian Ocean. China's 'blue water' navy with a new class of nuclear submarines armed with intercontinental missiles is challenging the extant balance of power. China is investing far greater resources in the modernization of its armed forces in general and its navy in particular than India seems either willing to commit or capable of sustaining at present. China's increasingly sophisticated submarine fleet could eventually be one of the world's largest, and with the rapid strides it has made in submarines, ballistic missiles, and GPS-blocking technology, some are suggesting that China will increasingly have the capacity to challenge America.[6] Senior Chinese officials have indicated that China would be ready to build an aircraft carrier by the end of the decade, as this is seen as being indispensable to protecting Chinese interests in oceans.[7] The intention to develop carrier capability marks a shift away from the strategy of devoting the bulk of PLA's modernization to the goal of capturing Taiwan. Chinese military planners have now given the green light to the building of two new nuclear powered aircraft carriers. One aircraft carrier — the Kuznetsov class Varyag — has been acquired from Russia and us already being refitted, allowing for the possibility of three aircraft carriers by 2017.

With the rise in China's economic and political power there has been a commensurate growth in its profile in the Indian Ocean region. China is acquiring naval bases near crucial chokepoints in the Indian Ocean not only to serve its economic interests but also to enhance its strategic presence in the region. China realizes that its maritime strength will give it the strategic leverage that it needs to emerge as the regional hegemon and a potential superpower, and there is evidence to suggest that China is building up its maritime power in all dimensions.[8] China's growing dependence on maritime space and resources is reflected in the Chinese aspiration to expand its influence and to ultimately dominate the strategic environment of the Indian Ocean region. China's growing interest in establishing bases across the Indian Ocean region is a response to its perceived vulnerability, given the logistical constraints that it faces due to the distance of the Indian Ocean waters from its own area of operation. In addition, China is consolidating power over the South China Sea and the Indian Ocean with an eye on India, something that comes out clearly in a secret memorandum issued by the Director of the General Logistic Department of the PLA: "We can no longer accept the Indian Ocean as only an ocean of the Indians . . . We are taking armed conflicts in the region into account."[9]

China has deployed its Jin class submarines at a submarine base near Sanya at the southern tip of Hainan Island in the South China Sea, raising the alarm in India as the base is merely 1200 nautical miles from the Malacca Strait and will be China's closest access point to the Indian Ocean. The base also has an underground facility that can hide the movement of submarines, making them difficult to detect.[10] The concentration of strategic naval forces at Sanya will propel China towards a consolidation of its control over the surrounding Indian Ocean region. The presence of access tunnels at the mouth of the deep water base is particularly troubling for India as it will have strategic implications in the Indian Ocean region, allowing China to interdict shipping at the three crucial chokepoints in the Indian Ocean. As the ability of China's navy to project power in the Indian Ocean region grows, India is likely to feel even more vulnerable despite enjoying distinct geographical advantages in the region. China's growing naval presence in and around the Indian Ocean region is troubling for India as it restricts India's freedom to maneuver in the region. Of particular note is what has been termed as China's "string of pearls" strategy that has significantly expanded China's strategic depth in India's backyard.[11]

This "string of pearls" strategy of bases and diplomatic ties include the Gwadar port in Pakistan, naval bases in Burma, electronic intelligence gathering facilities on islands in the Bay of Bengal, funding for the construction of a canal across the Kra Isthmus in Thailand, a military agreement with Cambodia, and a build-up of forces in the South China Sea.[12] Some of the claims about the implementation of parts of this strategy have been exaggerated, as was the case with the Chinese naval presence in Burma. The Indian government, for example, had to concede in 2005 that reports of China turning the Coco Islands in Burma into a naval base were incorrect and that there were indeed no naval bases in Burma.[13] Yet the Chinese thrust into the Indian Ocean is gradually becoming more and more pronounced. The Chinese may not have a naval base in Burma but they are involved in the upgrading of infrastructure in the Coco Islands and may be providing some limited technical assistance to Burma. Given that almost 80 percent of China's oil passes through the Strait of Malacca, the country is reluctant to rely on US naval power for unhindered access to energy and so has decided to build up its naval power at "chokepoints" along the sea routes from the Persian Gulf to the South China Sea. China is also courting other states in South Asia by building container ports in Bangladesh at Chittagong and in Sri Lanka at Hambantota. Consolidating its access to the Indian Ocean, China has signed an agreement with Sri Lanka to finance the development of the Hambantota Development Zone which includes a container port, a bunker system, and an oil refinery. It is possible to explain the construction of these ports and facilities around India's periphery by China in purely economic and commercial terms, but to India this looks like a policy of containment.

China's diplomatic and military efforts in the Indian Ocean seem to reflect a desire to project power vis-à-vis competing powers in the region such as the US and India. China's presence in the Bay of Bengal via roads and ports in Burma and in the Arabian Sea via the Chinese-built port of Gwadar in Pakistan has been a cause of concern for India. With access to crucial port facilities in Egypt, Iran, and Pakistan, China is well-poised to secure its interests in the region. China's involvement in the construction of the deep-sea port of Gwadar has attracted a lot of attention due to its strategic location, about 70 kilometers from the Iranian border and 400 kilometers east of the Strait of Hormuz, a major oil supply route. It has been suggested that it will provide China with a "listening post" from which it can "monitor US naval activity in the Persian Gulf, Indian activity in the Arabian Sea, and future US–Indian maritime cooperation in the Indian Ocean."[14] Though Pakistan's naval capabilities do not, on their own, pose any challenge to India, the combination of Chinese and Pakistani naval forces could indeed be formidable for India to counter.

It has been suggested that the Chinese government appears "to have a very clear vision of the future importance of the sea and a sense of the strategic leadership needed to develop maritime interests."[15] This is reflected in the attempts that China has made in recent years to build up all aspects of its maritime economy and to create one of the world's largest merchant fleets with a port, transport, and ship-building infrastructure to match. In this respect, the Indian Ocean has an important role to play in the Chinese efforts to establish itself as the main maritime power in the region. And this is resulting in Sino-Indian competition for influence in Indian Ocean and beyond. Despite a significant improvement in Sino-Indian ties since the late 1990s, the relationship remains competitive in nature, and by making use of its rising economic and military power, China has been successful in containing India within the confines of South Asia, particularly by building close ties with India's key neighbors, especially Pakistan.[16]

Yet, the notion that China aspires to naval domination of the Indian Ocean remains far-fetched. China would certainly like to play a greater role in the region, protect and advance its interests, especially Chinese commerce, as well as counter India. But given the immense geographical advantages that Indian enjoys in the Indian Ocean, China will have great difficulty in exerting as much sway in the Indian Ocean as India can. But all the steps that China is taking to protect and enhance its interests in the Indian Ocean region are generating apprehensions in Indian strategic circles about her real intentions, thereby engendering a classic security rivalry between the two Asian giants. And it is India's fears and perceptions of the growing naval power of China in the Indian Ocean that is driving Indian naval strategy. Tensions are inherent in such an evolving strategic relationship, as was underlined by an incident in January 2009 when an Indian Kilo class submarine and Chinese warships, on their way to the Gulf of Aden to patrol the pirate-infested waters, reportedly engaged in rounds of maneuvering to test for weaknesses in each other's sonar systems. The Chinese media reported that its warships forced the Indian submarine to surface, which was strongly denied by the Indian Navy.[17] Unless these situations are managed carefully, the potential for such incidents turning serious in the future remains high, especially as Sino-Indian naval competition is likely to intensify with the Indian and Chinese navies operating far from their shores.

The Indian Ocean: India's Backyard?

As India's global economic and political profile has risen in recent years, it has also, not surprisingly, tried to define its strategic interests in increasingly expansive terms. Like other globalizing economies, India is heavily reliant on the free flow of goods through the Indian Ocean SLOCs, especially as around 90 percent of India's trade depends on merchant shipping. Given India's growing reliance on imported sources of energy, any disruption in the Indian Ocean could have a potentially catastrophic impact on Indian economic and societal stability. India's Exclusive Economic Zone in the Indian Ocean, which according to the Law of the Seas runs 200 nautical miles out from its coastline and its islands, covers around 30 percent of the most resource abundant Indian Ocean Region.[18]

Any disruption in shipping on the important trade routes in the Indian Ocean, especially those passing through the "chokepoints" in the Strait of Hormuz, the Gulf of Aden, the Suez Canal, and the Strait of Malacca, would have serious consequences for not only India but also for global economic prospects. Unhindered trade and shipping traffic flow is a *sine qua non* for India's development. Non-traditional threats in the form of organized crime, piracy, and international terrorist networks also make it imperative for India to exert its control in the region.

Indian strategic thinkers have historically viewed the Indian Ocean as India's backyard and so have emphasized the need for India to play a greater role in underwriting its security and stability. India's strategic elites have often drawn inspiration from a quote attributed to Alfred Mahan: "Whoever controls the Indian Ocean dominates Asia. The ocean is the key to seven seas. In the twenty-first century, the destiny of the world will be decided on its waters." This quote, though apparently fictitious, has been highly influential in shaping the way Indian naval thinkers have looked at the role of the Indian Ocean for Indian security.[19] While parts of the Indian foreign policy establishment considered India the legatee of the British rule for providing peace and stability in the Indian Ocean, India's neighbors remain concerned about India's "hegemonistic" designs in the region.

Underlining the importance of Indian Ocean for India, K.M. Pannikar, a diplomat and historian, called for the Indian Ocean to remain "truly Indian." He argued that "to other countries the Indian Ocean could only be one of the important oceanic areas, but to India it is a vital sea because its lifelines are concentrated in that area, its freedom is dependent on the freedom of that coastal surface."[20] Pannikar was strongly in favor of Indian dominance of the Indian Ocean region, much as several British and Indian strategists viewed

India's dominance of the Indian Ocean as virtually inevitable.[21] It has also been suggested that given the role of "status and symbolism" in Indian strategic thinking, India's purported greatness would be reason enough for Indian admirals to demand a powerful navy.[22]

In view of this intellectual consensus, it is surprising that India's civilian leadership was able to resist naval expansion in the early years after independence. India took its time after independence to accept her role as the pre-eminent maritime power in the Indian Ocean region, and long remained diffident about shouldering the responsibilities that come with that status. The focus remained on Pakistan and China, and the overarching continental mindset continued to dictate the defense priorities of the nation, with some complaining that the Indian navy was being relegated to the background as the most neglected branch of the armed services.[23] As the great powers became involved in the Indian Ocean during the Cold War years, India's ability to shape developments in the region was further marginalized. India continued to lag behind in its ability to project power across the Indian Ocean through the early 1990s, primarily due to resource constraints and the lack of a clear strategy. It was rightly observed that "if the Indian Navy seriously contemplates power projection missions in the Indian Ocean, [then the Indian naval fleet] is inadequate . . . it has neither the balance nor the required offensive punch to maintain zones of influence."[24] India, for its part, continued to demand, without much success, that "extra-regional navies" withdraw from the Indian Ocean; these demands met with hostility from the major powers and generated apprehensions in India's neighborhood that India was seeking to dominate the strategic landscape of the Indian Ocean. India's general non-aligned foreign policy posture also ensured that Indian maritime intentions remained shrouded in mystery for the rest of the world.

It has only been since the late 1990s that India has started to reassert itself in the Indian Ocean and beyond. This has been driven by various factors: the high rates of economic growth that India has enjoyed since early 1990s have allowed the country to invest greater resources in naval expansion; the growing threat from non-state actors has forced India to adopt a more pro-active naval posture; and a growing realization that China is rapidly expanding its influence in the Indian Ocean region, something that many in the Indian strategic community feel would be detrimental to Indian interests in the long term. India has a pivotal position in the Indian Ocean, as unlike other nations in the region with blue-water capabilities such as Australia and South Africa, India is at the center and dominates the sea lanes of communication across the ocean in both directions. There are now signs that India is making a concerted effort to enhance its capabilities in support of its aspiration to play an enhanced naval role in the Indian Ocean.

India Responds to the Chinese Challenge

The augmentation of China's capabilities in the Indian Ocean has alarmed India and has galvanized it into taking ameliorative measures. Underscoring India's discomfort with China's "string of pearls" strategy, a former Indian naval chief has argued that "each pearl in the string is a link in a chain of the Chinese maritime presence" and has expressed concern that naval forces operating out of ports established by the Chinese could "take control over the world energy jugular."[25] India views Chinese naval strategy as expansionist and intent on encircling India strategically. Current Indian naval strategy is being driven by the idea "that the vast Indian Ocean is its *mare nostrum* . . . that the entire triangle of the Indian Ocean is their nation's rightful and exclusive sphere of interest."[26] Just as the PLA Navy seems to be concentrating on anti-access warfare to be able to prevent the US Navy from entering into a cross-Straits conflict, the Indian Navy is working to acquire the ability to deny China access to the Indian Ocean.[27] While the Indian Maritime Doctrine of 2004 underlined "attempts by China to strategically encircle India," the Indian Maritime Strategy released three years later emphasized attempts by the Chinese Navy to emerge as a blue-water force by pursuing an ambitious modernization program, "along with attempts to gain a strategic toe-hold in the Indian Ocean Rim."[28]

India's projection of naval power into the Indian Ocean and beyond is an outcome of India's increasingly outward-looking foreign policy, which is in line with its growing economic prowess. Through joint exercises, port visits, and disaster relief missions, the Indian Navy has dramatically raised its profile in the Indian Ocean region in the last few years. India's rapid response to the December 2004 tsunami was the largest relief mobilization ever by its naval forces and underlined its growing role in the Indian Ocean as well as its ability to be a net provider of security in the region. India was one of the few nations affected by the tragedy that was able to respond relatively effectively and lend a helping hand to neighboring countries by sending its naval ships and personnel. The Indian Navy also demonstrated its rapid response capability when it evacuated a large number of Indians and other nationals from Lebanon during the 2006 Israel–Lebanon conflict.

Diplomatic Initiatives

India is using its naval forces to advance its diplomatic initiatives overseas, and in particular to shape the strategic environment in and around the Indian Ocean. Indian interests converge with those of the US in the Indian Ocean region and it is trying to use the present upswing in US–India ties to create a more favorable strategic environment for itself in the region, despite its historical sensitivities to the presence of US forces in the Indian Ocean.[29] The US has also recognized the importance of India's role in the region, as was evident in Colin Powell's contention that it was important for the US to support India's role in maintaining peace and stability in the Indian Ocean and its vast periphery.[30] In its first maritime service strategy update in twenty-five years, the US indicated that it views its sea power as the primary instrument in the US defense arsenal to deter conflict with China, and cooperation with other countries' naval services, including India's, is recognized as crucial to fulfilling the US strategic imperatives in the region.[31] The US and Indian navies have stepped up their joint exercises and the US has sold India the USS *Trenton* (renamed INS *Jalashwa*), the first of its class to be inducted into the Indian Navy and an acquisition that marks a milestone in the US–India bilateral ties. The US would like India to join its Container Security Initiative (CSI) and Proliferation Security Initiative (PSI), but India remains reluctant. The PSI is viewed as a US-led initiative outside the United Nations mandate, while the CSI would result in the presence of US inspectors in Indian ports, making Indian participation politically impossible. However, India has indicated that it would be willing to join the US-proposed 1000-ship navy effort to combat illegal activities on the high seas, given the informal nature of the arrangement.[32] India is seen a balancer in the Asia-Pacific where US influence has waned in relative terms while China's has risen. India's ties with Japan have also assumed a new dynamic, with some even mooting a "concert of democracies" proposal involving the democratic states of the Asia-Pacific working towards their common goals of a stable Asia-Pacific region.[33] While such a proposal has little chance of evolving into anything concrete in the near term, especially given China's sensitivities, India's decision to develop natural gas with Japan in the Andaman Sea and recent military exercises involving the US, Japan, India, and Australia, do give a sense of India's emerging priorities.[34]

India's decision to establish its Far Eastern Command in the Andaman and Nicobar Islands in the Bay of Bengal is aimed at countering China's growing presence in the region by complicating China's access through the Strait of Malacca, the main passage point of oil bound for China. India has launched Project Seabird whose centerpiece is India's third operational naval base in Karwar on the nation's western seaboard, which consists of an air force station, a naval armament depot, and missile silos, aimed at securing the nation's maritime routes in the Arabian Sea.[35] India is set to establish a monitoring station in Madagascar, its first in another country, as it is deemed vital to guard against the terrorist threat emanating from East Africa as well as to keep an eye on China's activities in the region. India is also interested in developing a monitoring facility on an atoll in Mauritius and has strengthened its naval contacts with Mozambique and Seychelles. India responded to the Chinese President Hu Jintao's offer of military assistance to the Seychelles by donating one of its patrol aircraft to the Seychelles Navy. India's support in the building of Chahbahar port in Iran as well as the road connecting it to Afghanistan is an answer to the Chinese-funded Gwadar port in Pakistan. India's air base in Kazakhstan and its space monitoring post in Mongolia are also geared primarily towards China.

Competition between China and India is also increasing for influence in Burma as the Andaman Sea off Burma's coast is viewed as crucial energy lifeline for China, while India also needs Burma in order to meet its energy requirements. India will be rebuilding Burma's western Sittwe port and is one of the main suppliers of military hardware to the ruling junta. China's growing penetration of Burma is one of the main reasons India is reluctant to cease its economic and military engagement with the Burmese junta, despite the widespread criticism it has faced both from outside and within India.

India's "Look East" policy, originally aimed at strengthening economic ties with India's Southeast Asian neighborhood, has now led to naval exercises with Singapore, Thailand, and Indonesia. The member states of the Association of South-East Asian Nations (ASEAN) have joined the Indian Navy in policing the Indian Ocean region to curb piracy, smuggling, and other threats to sea-lanes. India has also accelerated its naval engagement with a number of Persian Gulf states, making port calls and conducting exercises with the navies of Kuwait, Oman, Bahrain, Saudi Arabia, Qatar, the United Arab Emirates, and Djibouti, as well as engaging with the navies of other major powers in the region such as the US, the UK, and France. It has also been suggested that to more effectively counter Chinese presence in the Indian Ocean and to protect its trade routes, India will have to seek access to Vietnamese, Taiwanese, and Japanese ports for the forward deployment of its naval assets.[36] India is already emerging as an exclusive "defense service provider" for smaller states with growing economies that seek to strengthen their military capabilities in Southeast Asia and West Asia, such as Vietnam, Indonesia, Malaysia, Singapore, Qatar, and Oman, providing it access to ports along the Arabian coast, Indian Ocean, and South China Sea.[37]

Naval Platforms and Doctrine

The Indian Navy is aiming for a total fleet of 140 to 145 vessels over the next decade, built around two carrier battle groups: *Admiral Gorshkov*, which will now be handed over to India in 2013, and the indigenous 37,500-ton STOBAR Air Defense Ship, likely to be completed by 2014. India's ambition to equip its navy with two or more aircraft carriers over the next decade, as well as its decision to launch its first indigenous nuclear submarine in 2009, are seen as crucial for power projection and to achieve a semblance of strategic autonomy. India's emerging capability to put a carrier task force as far from home as the South China Sea and the Persian Gulf has given a boost to the Indian Navy's blue-water aspirations and India hopes to induct a third aircraft carrier by 2017, ensuring that the Indian Navy has two operational carriers at all times.[38] The deployment of the Jin class submarine at Hainan by China will also force India to speed up its indigenous nuclear submarine project. This project has been in the pipeline for more than a decade now, with the Indian Navy rather ambitiously aiming for the induction of five indigenous ATV (Advanced Technology Vehicle) nuclear submarines. With the first trials of the submarine underway, India will be leasing an Akula II nuclear attack submarine from Russia for personnel training. A submarine-based nuclear arsenal is considered critical by Indian strategists to retain a second-strike capability. Despite some attempts at diversification, India's dependence on Russia for military equipment remains acute and has resulted in bilateral tension in recent times. The Indian military, in particular, has been critical of an over-reliance on Russia for defense acquisition, which was reflected in the Indian naval chief's view that India's ties with Russia should be rethought in light of the Russian demand of an additional $1.2 billion for the aircraft carrier, *Admiral Gorshkov*, which was purchased by India in 2004.[39] The Indian Navy is now actively looking to other states, particularly the US, for its new acquisitions.

While a focus on augmenting its platforms, systems, and weapons is clearly visible in the Indian Navy, concomitant changes in doctrine and organization have been relatively slow to emerge. It was only in 2004 that India published its first maritime doctrine since it gained its independence. The country's determination to establish its dominance in the Indian Ocean region comes across very clearly in this document. The maritime doctrine underlines four roles for the Indian Navy: military/strategic; political; constabulary; and benign agent of humanitarian assistance. The doctrine emphasizes the shift for the Indian Navy from conventional combat to include non-traditional threats and underscores the role of the Indian Navy in the nation's trade and energy policies. The doctrine calls for exercising control of the seas in designated areas of the Arabian Sea and the Bay of Bengal, and urges the navy to contribute towards strengthening India's credible nuclear deterrent in the form of nuclear submarines equipped with nuclear missiles. It emphasizes Indian concerns about growing Chinese naval capabilities by underlining the fact that China allocates 24 percent of its defense outlays to its navy compared to 16 percent in India's case, and describes Chinese plans to configure its force around two-carrier groups. The doctrine is a very ambitious document for a service that has always complained about lack of resources, yet it does not seem to offer a clear vision for the future. The challenge for the Indian Navy in the coming years will be to synergize its doctrine effectively with force planning and acquisitions.

Organizational changes in the armed forces of India have been even less visible. It has become imperative for the three services to cooperate more closely if the desired effects are to be achieved in contemporary warfare. "Jointery" or "Jointness" is the new buzz-word and the distinctions between sea, land, and air are becoming increasingly unimportant in expeditionary operations. Integration is essential not only for operational effectiveness but also as a force multiplier and a tool to achieve efficiency. And in this era of "joint-ness" of all the major armed forces in the world, India is probably the only one that is not fully integrated. India has taken some small steps towards uniting its armed forces, but inter-service rivalry continues to plague Indian defense forces. The Indian Army continues to insist that it should be seen as the most important element in the armed forces, while the Navy and Air Force continue to resent and resist the domination of the Army. The result is that while an Integrated Defense Staff has been set up, the move towards a Chief of Defense Staff has come to naught as the inter-service bickering gives the government an excuse to drag its feet with regard to the streamlining of decision-making on defense issues. Lack of cooperation among the three services has also led to duplication of purchases, hindering efficient utilization of precious resources, and the acquisition and procurement processes continue to remain extremely complex and opaque. India's much-hyped defense modernization program is suffering because of delays in the procurement of major weapon systems.

Conclusion

Both China and India would most certainly like to acquire the ability to project power and operate independently far from their shores. Yet currently it is China that seems more willing to commit to the expense of building up its fleet with a clear strategic agenda regarding how its wants to utilize its naval assets. The ability of Indian policy-makers to think strategically on national security and defense issues has been questionable at best. Ad hoc decision-making has been the norm, leading to a situation where long-time observers of India argue that it is likely that "India will be among the medium powers . . . a country of great economic capabilities but limited cultural and military influence."[40] With policy-makers in New Delhi far removed from the nation's sea frontiers, there is a poor understanding of maritime issues. This political apathy has led to the nation's armed forces operating in a strategic void. The Indian Navy's attempt to come up with its own strategy and doctrine, though welcome in many respects, has little meaning in the absence of a national security strategy from the Indian government.

Asia is witnessing the simultaneous rise of two giants, China and India, and this will inevitably cause some international complications. It has been suggested that Sino-Indian relations in the Indian Ocean are beset by mutual suspicion and insecurity similar to those that characterized the Japanese-American rivalry in the Pacific during the first half of the twentieth century over SLOCs.[41] While the cost of not cooperating will be high for both China and India, the struggle for power and influence between the Asian giants will continue to shape India's naval posture as well as the strategic environment of the Indian Ocean region in the coming years.

5

China in the Middle East
Balancing the Applecart

US power and influence in the Middle East is under threat. The prolonged conflicts in Iraq and Afghanistan, failure to resolve the Israeli–Palestinian conflict, and broader geo-political dynamics have weakened the hegemonic grip of the United States on the region and served to strengthen other actors on the international stage. China, recognized to be an emerging economic superpower, may use its economic strength to create a central role for itself on the international political stage in the future. This chapter examines Chinese priorities in the Middle East and assesses whether these will lead China to fill this potential emerging power vacuum.

China has a number of strategic priorities that shape its current role in the international system. Its primary interest is to continue its present pace of economic development and to maintain the global strategic balance of power which has so far served Chinese interests so well. Alongside its economic development program, China has invested in a broad military modernization program that aims to turn the country into a military power commensurate with China's growing economic strength. Politically, China has avoided complicated foreign entanglements that would jeopardize its economic interests, but has nevertheless been raising its profile and playing a more active role on the international stage than it has in the past.

China's rapid economic growth drives a growing need for energy imports that has made the Middle East a central focus of its foreign policy. Since the 1980s China has sought to strengthen its relations with key regional energy suppliers, particularly Iran and Saudi Arabia. It has also strengthened ties with Israel in order to import the advanced weapons technology necessary for its military modernization program. In recent years China has been more willing to take advantage of the relative decline in US influence in the region to advance its economic interests, and it has courted rogue regimes and militant groups hostile to Israel and the US. However, it courts these regimes primarily in order to secure the use of their economic resources, and only so long as they do not significantly jeopardize the security and stability of the region as a whole. It is neither willing, nor able, to take on the US role of playing power broker in the region. The Chinese challenge to US hegemony is subtle, and the moment the US or wider international community has pushed it, China has indicated a willingness to pull back. Its main priority in the Middle East is to maintain the balance of power that currently exists and tread delicately between the competing poles in the region so as not to jeopardize this overall stability.

This chapter explores China's policy priorities in the Middle East by analysing its relations with three key regional players that exemplify its broader engagement with the region today: Iran, Saudi Arabia, and Israel. It argues that China is primarily guided by economic interests and only takes a stand on political issues when it must do so in order to advance these interests. But there is little doubt that China's influence in the Middle East today is at an all time high.

China in the Middle East: A Historical Perspective

During the early years of the Cold War, China attempted to export its brand of revolutionary Communism throughout the Third World, including the Middle East, which was seen as a potentially fertile ground for radical ideologies. However, by the late 1960s it became clear that this was not a useful policy as it deflected attention from China's primary goal of economic development. Contrary to expectations, the policy proved particularly ineffective in the Middle East, where most states relied so heavily on superpower patrons that they had little room for forging alliances with other non-essential external actors. Another factor that complicated Chinese diplomatic aims in the region was that most Middle Eastern states were also already well disposed towards Taiwan and would not abandon this alliance for the sake of building relations with China.

As the Cold War continued into the 1970s, Sino-US relations thawed, with President Nixon visiting the Peoples Republic of China (PRC) in 1972. As a result, China developed ties with those

Middle Eastern states that were suspicious of Soviet involvement in the region. While developing these new alliances, China continued to use rhetoric to project itself as a leader of the Third World above the geo-political rivalry of the two superpowers. However this posture was largely symbolic, as by the late 1970s China's main concern was economic development, and it would not consider radical policy initiatives that jeopardized this goal. The end of the Cold War and the collapse of the Soviet Empire saw China emerge as a major global economic player as well as the remaining bastion of communism. However for many years following China's economic boom in the late 1980s, it did not play the kind of active role in international affairs that would seem to have been commensurate with its economic weight. This was primarily because the Chinese political leadership had made a strategic choice to emphasize economic development at home without attempting to play a more interventionist global role.[1] China also remained a very closed country with a communist leadership not prepared to allow easy access for diplomats or the media.

China's Strategic Priorities

In recent years China has become more ambitious in defining its foreign strategic agenda. Today it is primarily concerned with maintaining global stability, seen as essential for ensuring China's long-term economic development. As a result, China has been expanding its presence and deepening its engagement with states in all parts of the world beyond the Asia-Pacific, including the Middle East. This newfound foreign engagement is driven by three overarching strategic priorities that influence Chinese foreign policy-making today.

1. Economics and energy

China's primary concern is economic development and its increasing energy requirements. Its newfound engagement in various regions around the world is driven by the realization that an active international role is necessary in order to maintain its current economic trajectory of double-digit growth rates. While much of the Western world is now trying to reduce reliance on oil, seeking alternative energy sources, China is wholly reliant on oil because of the significant role that heavy industry plays in its booming economy. A significant proportion of the oil and other natural resources needed to run the economy are imported by China, and so wooing nations that are rich in energy and other raw materials became of paramount importance. For three decades after the 1949 establishment of the People's Republic, energy concerns were only a minor factor in Beijing's national security assessment as China's main oilfield in Daqing was producing enough oil to meet national demand.[2] However, as China's economy developed, its dependence on external oil began to grow, and by 1993 China had become a net importer of oil, with a demand of 5.5 million barrels per day. In 2003 China surpassed Japan to become the world's second largest oil consumer after the US.[3]

2. Military

Since the late 1970s, the government has launched a program to modernize the country's Peoples Liberation Army (PLA). The army is 2.3 million strong (the world's largest active standing army) but technologically limited. The Chinese government has long argued that the main motivation for this modernization drive is the need to posses a military capability commensurate with its economic strength. China has borders with fifteen Asian countries, some of which seem to pose a threat to regional stability, including Taiwan, North Korea, Pakistan, and India. China's official defense expenditure is now around 1.5 percent of its GDP, and China's GDP has been growing at over 10 percent every year. China's military expenditure grew by 12 percent in 2006, and China emerged as the biggest military spender in the region, and the fourth largest in the world.[4] Its military modernization program has made China one of the largest weapons importers in the world and its foreign policy priorities have been calibrated accordingly.[5] China has a burgeoning appetite for arms and has developed and nurtured alliances all over the world in order to secure the defense contracts that are crucial for advancing its military modernization program.

3. Political

There has recently been much debate over China's role in the global diplomatic and political arena. Its growing engagement and expanding interests in many regions across the world have meant that China has been at the forefront of debates on many pressing global political issues, such as the conflicts in Burma and Sudan, in which it previously had little or no stake. China has a permanent seat on the UN Security Council and is increasingly using this status to challenge Western priorities. Its crucial role in any strategy to tackle climate change has meant that it is given center stage in political forums debating this increasingly urgent global issue. In opening its doors to the world by hosting the Olympic Games in 2008, China has been forced to address the diplomatic ramifications of its policies in Tibet. China has demonstrated its willingness and ability to play a central role on all fronts in the global arena and has engaged at every level with the political policy-making that comes with such a role.

Nonetheless, relative to its economic strength, China is still a relatively passive player in the international community. Its primary diplomatic focus is the issue of Taiwan, and it has generally shied away from unnecessary political entanglements that would complicate this matter. China does not seek open confrontation with the United States, as its relatively cooperative relations with the US are seen as key to maintaining the current balance of power in the global system that has so far served Chinese economic interests.

Driving Interests in the Middle East

Chinese interests in the Middle East reflect its overarching global priorities, and its engagement with the region is focused on securing its economic interests and expanding the markets in which it can sell arms. China's relatively narrow political ambitions are reflected in its policy of diplomatic balancing between the various poles and actors in the region.

1. Energy

Energy security for China is crucial to sustain its present rate of economic growth, and the Middle East is the backbone of Chinese energy policy worldwide. Today more than 51 percent of China's oil imports originate in the Persian Gulf and it has been estimated that by 2030, the Gulf will supply one in every three barrels of China's consumption.[6] China's appetite for oil will only grow in the coming years and its dependence on Middle Eastern sources of energy is set to increase. Saudi Arabia and Iran account for around 30 percent of China's oil imports, and these two countries have therefore emerged as the main focus of China's Middle East policy.[7] Even in Iraq Chinese companies now enjoy stakes in three of the eleven contracts signed by the Iraqi Oil Ministry, and Beijing successfully renegotiated a $3 billion deal that was signed with Saddam Hussein's regime in 1997 to develop the Iraqi oil fields of al-Ahdab. China is now the leading oil and gas investore in Iraq.

2. Arms

Another main driver of Chinese economic interests in the region is the need to secure a stable market for its arms exports and to import advanced weapons technology to strengthen its own arms manufacturing industry. Israel has been one of China's major sources of advanced weapons systems, as China has made use of Israeli advanced military technology as a way of circumventing the EU and US arms embargo imposed on it following the 1989 massacre in Tiananmen Square. China has also used its "no questions asked" policy on arms sales as a way of increasing and securing access to Middle Eastern energy markets, with Tehran, the world's second largest oil producer, emerging as the second-largest buyer of Chinese military hardware: the country has accounted for almost 14 percent of Chinese military exports between 2005 and 2009.[8] And China's sale of weaponry to the new government in Baghdad already exceeds $100 million.

3. Politics and diplomacy

While maintaining its focus on economic priorities, China has become increasingly disposed to take advantage of the relative decline of US influence in the region in the past few years. Long-term trends that are emerging point to a possible power vacuum in the Middle East which China could potentially capitalize on. China also has a history of opposing hegemony and of using the rhetoric of preserving the equality of nations in the international system.[9] This has encouraged China to court rogue regimes and challenge US dominance when the opportunity arises.

However, the interests of Washington and Beijing converge on a wide range of issues pertaining to the region, and China is not willing or able to disturb this relative balance and jeopardize their common interests. America has special ties with almost all major states in the region and the US military plays a crucial role in maintaining the strategic balance of power. Chinese policy makers are well aware that they lack the resources and political capital to be the kind of stabilizing force in the region that the US has been in recent years, and they restrict their policy goals accordingly. The only occasions when China has openly stood up to the US are when it has strengthened its ties with a country in order to further its economic interests in the region, rather than because of any broader global power ambitions. In such cases, China usually offers the country diplomatic protection from the US as an incentive for strengthening their bilateral economic ties.

4. The Islamic linkage

Another factor that impacts Chinese policy in the region is its relationship with its Muslim population and fear of Islamist extremism. China has a seven-million-strong restive Muslim population in the resource-rich western province of Xinjiang. The Uighurs, who have been trying to preserve their distinct cultural identity in the face of Chinese influence, have openly displayed their dissatisfaction with the Chinese government, occasionally resorting to violence. The most recent incident was an attempt in 2008 by a Uighur suicide bomber to blow up a plane from Xinjiang en route to Beijing. One of the ways in which China has tried to quell unrest in this Muslim-dominated region is by building ties with Middle Eastern states that are the ideological center of Islam. States such as Iran and Saudi Arabia have been active in propagating their version of Islam across the globe by providing resources and training to various organizations. China feels that it is necessary to have their support if it wants to successfully tackle Uighur insurgency, even though it is primarily in the Central and South Asian states that Uighur militants have found support. The silence of the Middle Eastern states regarding the Chinese government's attitude towards its Muslim population perhaps indicates a measure of success that China has achieved in keeping this issue under control.

Iran

China's relationship with Iran shows how its policy towards the

Middle East is driven almost exclusively by economic self-interest. China has sought to tread a careful path, pursuing its desire to expand its lucrative energy, arms, and nuclear deals while being careful to avoid seriously undermining its relations with the rest of the international community, which has been at loggerheads with Iran over its nuclear program. China's voting record in the United Nations Security Council demonstrates its unwillingness to offer substantial support to Iran's nuclear ambitions. Despite political grandstanding, it has not used its veto in any of the several rounds of United Nations sanctions against Iran, evidence that, at least for now, Chinese interests lie closer to Washington than Tehran.

China's need for energy remains the central focus of its relationship with Iran, the world's second-largest oil producer. The growing economic ties between the two countries make this relationship one of the most important China has in the region. In 2004 the former Iranian oil minister, Bijan Namdar Zanganeh, expressed Tehran's wish to see China become its largest oil and gas importer, a wish that China fulfilled by the end of that year. Today, Iranian oil accounts for at least 14 percent of China's total oil imports, up from just 1 percent in 1994, and Iran is second only to Saudi Arabia as a supplier of oil to China.[10]

In an effort to ensure their long-term energy security, China and Iran have engaged in a number of large oil and gas projects to develop existing Iranian capacity. An agreement signed in 2004 between former Iranian oil minister Bijan Namdar Zanga and China's National Reform and Development Commission committed China to buying 250 million tons of Iranian oil over the next twenty-five years in exchange for the development of Iran's Yadavaran oilfield. Natural gas is another major area of Sino-Iranian trade, exemplified by the Chinese-government-owned Zhuhai Zhenrong Corporation's $20 billion deal to buy 110 million tons of natural gas from Iran over the next 25 years starting in 2008.[11]

While securing access to Iranian energy is the main focus of China's relationship with Iran, Tehran is also the largest single market for Chinese arms, purchasing a total of $200 million worth from 2001 to 2004.[12] China has sold several hundred Silkworm anti-ship cruise missiles to Iran since the late 1980s and has been Iran's major source of missile guidance equipment and technology since the early 1990s. The sale of advanced weapon systems such as anti-ship missiles to Iran and the subsequent reappearance of these weapons in the hands of Iranian-backed militant groups such as Hezbollah has been widely condemned by the international community and is a source of tension between China, the US, and Israel.[13]

The most controversial area of Sino-Iranian defense ties has been China's cooperation with Iran's nuclear program, to which China has supplied dual-use missile-related items, raw materials, weapons-related production equipment, and technology.[14] China has openly defied demands by the US and the wider international community that it take a tougher stance against Iranian nuclear proliferation. China's voting record at the United Nations Security Council demonstrates that although it has never voted against sanctions, it has been prepared, together with Russia, to use its influence to water down tougher sanctions proposals.[15] Ultimately China will not jeopardize its relationships with the West to defend its trading partners in the Middle East. While it has gone along with sanctions, it has also made sure that energy imports and exports were kept off the United Nations list.

Energy is driving China's relationship with Iran, and the two countries are collaborating on a number of major energy projects, but the Sino-Iranian relationship dates back to the 1980s when China started supplying Tehran arms. The list of the arms supplied by China to Iran has expanded from cruise missiles to long-range ballistic missiles and assistance with Iran's chemical and nuclear weapons program. Iran hopes to overcome its global isolation by courting China, and China can make use of Iran's energy resources without any real competition. Chinese firms are key suppliers of ballistic and cruise missile technologies to Iran as Iran is China's main customer in the region both for conventional arms sales and for weapons of mass destruction.[16] China is also helping Iran develop a nuclear fuel cycle for civil and nuclear weapon purposes, despite Beijing's 1997 bilateral commitment to the US to forgo any new nuclear cooperation with Iran. China has made sure that the West is unable to take any effective coercive measures against Iran on the issue of its nuclear program even as Iran has continued to ignore the Security Council resolutions. Although the United Nations has been taking measures against Iran for several years now, China, a permanent member of the Security Council, has been able to pursue its energy interests with Iran without much difficulty. China is now the only major economy with significant investments in Iran's energy sector. More troublingly, despite sanctions, the Chinese firms continue to help Iran in improving its missile technology and developing nuclear weapons. Chinese firms have been discovered selling high-quality carbon fiber to Iran to help its build better centrifuges, used in enriching uranium.[17]

However, as international concern over Iran's nuclear program grows, China's efforts to prevent the passage of really tough sanctions could become an increasingly thorny problem for the international community.

Saudi Arabia

Much as in the case of Iran, Chinese relations with Saudi Arabia are mainly driven by oil, and the Chinese government has recently worked hard to improve its ties with the Kingdom. In 2004 China's state oil company, SINOPEC, signed a deal to explore for gas in Saudi Arabia's vast Empty Quarter (Rub al-Khali). In December 2005, Beijing held its first formal talks with the Organization of Petroleum Exporting Countries (OPEC) in an effort to guarantee a framework that would continue to meet China's growing demand for oil. The visit by Saudi King Abdullah bin Abdul Aziz to China in January 2006, his first visit abroad as king and the first by a Saudi monarch to China, demonstrated the deepening ties between the world's fastest growing oil market and the world's biggest oil supplier.

Saudi Arabia is China's leading trading partner in the region, while China is Saudi Arabia's fourth-largest trading partner. Bilateral trade between China and Saudi Arabia registered annual growth rates of 30 to 50 percent between 2003 and 2008. In 2008, bilateral trade surged to $41.8 billion, two years ahead of the goal set in 2006. It is expected that bilateral trade volume will exceed the goal set by the two nations of $60 billion by 2015. China's crude oil imports from Saudi Arabia rose by over 12 percent in 2009 to 800,000 barrels per day.[18] Over 17 percent of Chinese oil imports originate in Saudi Arabia, making it China's largest crude oil supplier.[19] China and Saudi Arabia have a symbiotic investment relationship in the oil sector and Saudi Arabia has emerged as a major investor in Chinese refineries. The Saudi company ARAMCO announced in July 2005 that it was investing $3.5 billion in a refinery expansion project in China's Fujian province to enable the plant to handle high-sulfur Saudi crude oil, and it is constructing another $1.2 billion refinery in Qingdao with China's state oil company, SINOPEC.[20]

Arms sales are another key aspect of the Sino-Saudi relationship. Since the 1980s, China has used the sale of advanced weapons systems and military technology as a way of gaining greater access to Saudi Arabia's oil market. A number of high-profile arms deals have however been highly contentious, in particular the 1987 sale of fifty Chinese CSS-2 nuclear-capable, intermediate-range ballistic missiles. This greatly alarmed the international community and at the time stoked increasing fears of missile proliferation, contributing to the 1987 Missile Technology Control Regime (MTCR) which China subsequently agreed to adhere to. Riyadh has more recently preferred to limit the quantity and type of weapons it buys from China in order to maintain its close ties with the US, Saudi Arabia's largest arms provider, and China has done little to try and divert Saudi Arabia from this course.

China's policy towards Saudi Arabia is dominated by its drive to secure long-term energy interests without becoming overtly entangled in the regions' complicated politics. US relations with Saudi Arabia are key to maintaining stability in the Middle East, and China understands that securing its long-term energy interests in the region necessitates increasing cooperation with the US, rather than competing with it.

Israel

In light of China's growing closeness to Iran and the Arab world, it is interesting that China has been able to maintain positive bilateral relations with Israel. The main driving factor in this relationship is economics, and neither party is willing to compromise on lucrative bilateral trade because of symbolic political posturing.

The most significant of these economic ties are in the area of defense. China is a huge market for Israeli defense equipment. The US and EU arms embargo on China means that the country is heavily dependent on Israeli arms as a means to acquire US-made weapons platforms to underpin its ambitious military modernization program.[21] Israel emerged as China's largest defense supplier after Russia in the early 1990s.[22] Since the establishment of diplomatic relations in 1992, bilateral Sino-Israeli trade has grown dramatically, and in 2009 bilateral trade between the two countries exceeded $5 billion.[23] China has become one of Israel's leading trade partners and the third largest exporter to the country (following the United States and Germany).[24]

Ties between China and Israel have at times been strained because of US pressure on Israel to limit the extent of its defense cooperation with China. In July 2000 American pressure resulted in Israel canceling the Chinese order for a Phalcon early warning aircraft because the deal was perceived as contrary to American national security interests. Similar tensions emerged in 2004–5 when Israel sought to obtain contracts from China to upgrade Israeli-manufactured HARPY drones (unmanned aircraft). Again the technology involved in this weapons system was deemed sensitive by Washington, and its export to China contrary to national security interests. However, despite these strains on the relationship, Israel and China continue to develop close economic ties and advance their arms trading where possible.

These strong economic ties are reinforced by continuing close diplomatic relations. Up until 1956, Israel was the only country in the Middle East to recognize the People's Republic of China, and Israel has been careful never to grant diplomatic recognition to Taiwan. The diplomatic closeness between Israel and China has been symbolized by a number of high-level visits and delegations. Every Israeli president since Chaim Herzog, as well as prime ministers Yitzhak Rabin, Benjamin Netanyahu, Ariel Sharon, and Ehud Olmert, have visited China. In January 2007 Olmert traveled to China for his first official visit since becoming prime minister and described his meeting with President Hu Jintao as "satisfactory beyond expectation." The visit was an opportunity to promote bilateral economic relations and sign new commercial and investment agreements for joint research and development funds. Israel was also given permission to open a third official office in Guangdong province, making Israel's present level of diplomatic representation in the PRC second only to its representation in the US.[25]

Chinese relations with Israel do not however operate in a vacuum, and have at times been strained because of China's policy towards Iran, its public support for Palestinian militant groups, and its supply of arms to Israel's enemies. However, China has, at crucial junctures, proved itself unwilling to compromise its lucrative economic ties with Israel because of disagreements over regional policy, nor has it been willing to suffer the difficulties with the US that would result from its being seen to jeopardize the security of one of its closest allies in the region.

In the case of Iran, China has selectively cooperated with the international community's efforts to isolate Iran and force it to cease enriching uranium. In a show of Israeli gratitude for Chinese cooperation, Olmert scheduled a visit to Beijing in January 2007, shortly after China had agreed to a third round of sanctions. Olmert said that during the visit he received candid reassurance from Chinese officials that the country opposes any plans by Iran to develop nuclear weapons, and China's official news agency, Xinhua, quoted Prime Minister Wen as telling Olmert that the country "will continue to play a constructive role in promoting the settlement of the [Iran] issue."

China is also a vocal supporter of the Palestinian cause. Most recently, China has taken steps to build ties with Hamas, inviting the then Palestinian Foreign Minister, Mahmud al-Zahar, a member of Hamas, to the China–Arab Forum in 2006, much to the consternation of Israel and the West.[26] However, this has not resulted in any significant material help being given to the Palestinians, and China's role in the peace process has always been limited. In the past, Beijing supported the Oslo agreements and the Israeli–Palestinian and Israel–Jordan peace processes; but it took only a very small role in promoting mediation and was a supportive bystander rather than an active participant. In a sign of increased assertiveness in the peace process, China appointed veteran diplomat Wang Shijie as its first Middle Eastern peace envoy in 2002. However, despite this gesture, China's role has remained largely symbolic and has not affected the course of Middle East peacemaking in any demonstrable way. In general China has not taken a very active role in the peace process, for fear of offending either side. Its involvement has always been largely rhetorical and has been an example of the delicate balancing act China plays between keeping its Arab and Iranian economic partners happy while maintaining fruitful relations with Israel and the US.

However, as China's economy continues to grow and its economic ties within the region deepen, there is scope for China to use its economic interests to play a more active role in the peace process. While it pledged only $11 million of the $7.4 billion promised at the International Donors Conference for Palestine in December 2007, China expressed a firm commitment to supporting the Palestinian economy, and Chinese Middle East envoy Sun

Bigan noted that "economic development in Palestine is closely connected with the region's political process." It is therefore in the indirect pursuit of greater economic engagement that China might begin to assume a more substantial diplomatic profile, with the potential to become a sponsor for peace in the region.

The one area where China remains defiant and continues to risk the wrath of some of its closest allies, including Israel, is its no-questions-asked arms sale policy. The war in Lebanon in the summer of 2006 highlighted the threat posed by China continuing to supply arms to countries like Iran and Syria, whose weapons were transferred to Hezbollah and then used against Israel. While China has seemed to bow to growing US-led pressure on it to cease assisting the Iranians in their nuclear enrichment program, it has shown no signs of tightening restrictions on the sale of conventional weapons to states that transfer them to rouge militant groups.

Conclusion: Where Does China Go From Here?

The rise of China is a reality that the major powers in the international system are adjusting to, and the Middle East, given its pivotal position in global politics, is likely to experience the impact of China's growing influence more than other regions. However, China's strategic objectives in the short to medium term remain focused on preserving stability in the region as Chinese aspirations for continued high rates of economic growth are best served by a stable Middle East with which to do business.

To date China has been very successful in achieving its regional economic objectives. It has developed strong partnerships with major powers such as Saudi Arabia, Iran, and Israel that will serve its energy and defense needs in the foreseeable future. It has been able to do this without having to make difficult diplomatic decisions, relying on the US to maintain regional stability. With the US facing challenges in the region, China's options for engagement have widened. Chinese policy-makers are reluctant, however, to raise their diplomatic profile too much for fear of compromising the delicate balancing act it has perfected.

A sustained engagement with China is the only way to test real Chinese intentions towards the region. It is unlikely that China will adopt a pro-active role either in the Middle East peace process or in the resolution of various immediate crises in Iran and Iraq in the near future. However, greater engagement with China, both formal and informal, on issues pertaining to the Middle East is important given its stake in the evolving strategic environment in the region.

The West, however, should be more assertive in holding China to account for its proliferation record in the region in both conventional and non-conventional weapons, particularly in light of its sale of ballistic missiles to Saudi Arabia and its sale of weapons to Iran which have been used by terrorist groups such as Hezbollah. Given that the biggest threat to global and regional security remains the danger of weapons of mass destruction falling into the hands of non-state actors, China's strict compliance with its non-proliferation commitments is a necessity that cannot be ignored.

It is unlikely that there will be a significant change in China's approach towards the region as long as its interests are served by remaining on good terms with all the key actors. China is reluctant to upset the diplomatic applecart it has so assiduously balanced since the early 1990s. The West should use China's broad diplomatic alliances not only to encourage China to do more to improve regional stability but also as a bridge to facilitate greater dialogue with those regimes in the Middle East that have been openly hostile to Western interests, such as Iran. But the West should not expect much, as China will be guided primarily by its economic interests in the region and would be reluctant to play a broader role in the short to medium term.

6

China in Africa
The Push Continues But All's Not Well

It almost seems as if Africa is the new El Dorado given the vigor with which the People's Republic of China seems to be pursuing the region. Top Chinese officials have been regularly visiting the continent for the last several years underscoring the solid commitment of the communist leadership to make China the principal external partner of the continent. In a significant move China organized the Forum on China–Africa Cooperation with great fanfare in November 2006 which was attended by the political leaders of forty-eight out of the fifty-three African countries.

It is not without significance that the superpower-in-waiting is asserting its growing political and economic power in a continent that has often felt neglected by other major global players. Concerns are rising in the West about China's growing prominence in Africa as the clout of former colonial powers such as Britain and France wanes and the US remains distracted with its domestic economic troubles and Islamist extremism. This chapter examines the growing Chinese engagement with the African continent and argues that despite the positive aspects of this relationship being emphasized by China, tensions are brewing beneath the surface as Africans are gradually beginning to realize the costs of their ties with China.

China's Rising Global Profile

In many ways, China's assertiveness in Africa should not be surprising. As China becomes more economically powerful, it is bound to adopt a more ambitious strategic agenda and assert itself across the globe. This is a trend that all great powers have followed throughout history.[1] China realizes that it has thrived because it devotes itself to economic development while letting the US police the region and the world.

For a long time, China shied away from playing the kind of active role in international affairs that would seem commensurate with its economic weight. This was primarily because the Chinese political leadership had made a strategic choice to concentrate on economic development at home without attempting to play a more interventionist role in global politics. But the last few years have seen China abandon this reticence and signal that it was no longer willing to watch events unfold from the sidelines, thereby accepting its new status as a significant global player. China is expanding its presence and deepening its engagement with states in all parts of the world including Africa.

There is also a realization in China that an active international role is necessary in order to maintain its current economic trajectory of double-digit growth rates. A significant proportion of the oil and other natural resources needed to run its economy are imported by China, and so wooing nations that are rich in energy and other raw materials has become of paramount importance. In this regard, Africa holds special significance. China is the second-largest consumer of oil in the world and one-third of China's total crude imports comes from Angola, Sudan, Congo, Gabon, Equatorial Guinea, Chad, and Nigeria.[2] Beijing's huge purchases of oil and other resources have made it Africa's third-largest economic partner, after the US and France. Angola is now the largest oil exporter to China, sidelining even Saudi Arabia. Moreover, China also has to keep searching for new markets for its burgeoning manufacturing sector. China is defending its interests in Africa through the time-tested means that have been employed by great powers, which include providing substantial economic assistance, subsidizing companies to help capture export markets, and politically supporting and selling arms to regimes that co-operate with it economically, even though they might be considered "rogue" by the rest of the world.

Politically, China intends to build diplomatic support among African nations for its priorities at the United Nations and other global institutions, where its interests are increasingly diverging from those of the West. While not overtly trying to countervail the US through internal defense build-ups or the formation of alliances, China, according to some, will try to use "soft balancing" to contain the US by entangling it in a web of international institutional rules and procedures or *ad hoc* diplomatic maneuvers.[3] China's growing engagement with Africa also helps it to further marginalize Taiwan as the number of states extending diplomatic recognition to Taiwan dwindles in Africa under Chinese pressure. A prerequisite for doing serious business with China is to recognize China and sever ties with Taiwan. In its first ever white paper on Africa, brought out in 2006, China asserted that if African states choose to accept the "one China principle as the potential foundation for the establishment and development of China's relationship with African countries," China will "co-ordinate positions on major international and regional issues and stand for mutual support on major issues concerning state sovereignty, territorial integrity, national dignity, and human rights."[4] Of the more than twenty African countries that recognized Taiwan in the early 1990s, only six now remain. China's success in luring states away from Taiwan has been remarkable, adding further to Taiwan's isolation in the international system in general and in Africa in particular.[5]

The Dragon Woos Africa

Throughout the Cold War, China's engagement with Africa had to take a back seat to the former Soviet Union's involvement in the region. Though China tried to project itself as a leader of the Third World and provided support to several left-wing regimes, it was the Soviets to whom the states in the region turned if they needed support against the West. Though China's foreign policy, for obvious reasons, took different forms in relation to different African states, its central focus through the early Cold War years was to support revolutionary movements in Africa, even though there was little possibility of the continent ever being swept by anti-imperialist and social revolutions of the kind the Chinese leadership propounded.[6] Over time, China's foreign policy towards Africa, despite its stated revolutionary aims, became evolutionary and pragmatic as trade became China's priority and African leaders became more tactful in their dealings with China, benefiting from its material aid and learning from its developmental trajectory.[7]

The structural constraints imposed by the Cold War disappeared in the early 1990s, and since then China has gradually tried to increase its clout in the region. In a rapidly evolving global strategic environment, cultivating economic and diplomatic ties with African nations has emerged as a major foreign policy priority for China in recent years. Trade between China and Africa is growing faster than with any other region except the Middle East, increasing tenfold over the past decade and crossing the $50 billion mark in 2006. From 2000 to 2008, China–Africa trade has enjoyed annual growth rates of more than 33 percent and reached a peak of $106.8 billion in 2008. After a mild dip due to the financial crisis the bilateral trade hit a record high of more than $110 billion in 2010.[8] Direct Chinese investment in Africa has already reached $6.6 billion, mostly in energy and infrastructure projects. China has extended African nations more than $1 billion in debt relief. Chinese companies have invested capital into a range of African projects in the last decade, from railways in Angola to telecommunications in Nigeria, and even hotels in Sierra Leone. This is part of a sustained wooing of Africa by China, led by its top decision-makers who have been regularly touring Africa, lobbying for lucrative contracts and promising investments.

As a sign of the seriousness with which the Chinese communist leadership has been taking its engagements in Africa recently, the Chinese foreign minister was in West Africa in January 2006; the Chinese President was in Nigeria, Morocco, and Kenya in April 2006; and the Chinese Prime Minister visited some seven African countries in June 2006. The year closed with the largest China–Africa gathering since the founding of Communist China in 1949, at which the Chinese and African leaders signed deals worth $1.9 billion, covering telecommunications, infrastructure, insurance, and mineral resources. Assurances from China that it would not monopolize Africa's resources as its increases its influence across the continent were also given. China also agreed to extend $1.5 billion in loans and credits to Africa, forgive past debts, and double foreign aid to the continent by 2009. China and the participating nations from Africa also declared a strategic partnership and "action plan" that charts co-operation in economic matters, international affairs, and social development.[9] The following year, 2007, again saw the Chinese President visiting Africa, including Cameroon, Liberia, Zambia, Namibia, South Africa, Mozambique, Sudan, and the Seychelles in his itinerary. Just before his visit, China announced that it would lend African nations $3 billion in preferential credit over the next three years as well as double aid and interest-free loans over the same time. It was emphasized that China's offer did not come with any political conditions attached to it. As he had during earlier visits, the Chinese President sought to boost economic ties, secure energy supplies, and find lucrative new investment opportunities for Chinese firms during his tour. Hu dispensed billions of dollars worth of debt relief, discounted loans, and facilitated new investments even as he signed various agreements opening Chinese markets to African agricultural products, a long-standing demand of the African states. This high-level Chinese engagement with Africa has continued unabated for the last three years.

China has also very shrewdly used its clout to secure business opportunities for its state-owned oil companies. China National Offshore Oil Corporation (CNOOC) has acquired a 45 percent stake in an oil block in Nigeria that started production in 2008. China used a $2 billion aid package to convince the Angolan government to sell a block auctioned by Shell in 2004, and lured Nigeria into providing 30,000 barrels of oil a day to PetroChina with an $800 million deal in 2005. The China National Petroleum Corporation (CNPC) is a joint venture with the Greater Nile Petroleum Operating Company which has invested over $8 billion in Sudan.[10] For many African nations, the most attractive aspect of Chinese involvement in their continent is its no-strings-attached aid policy. Aid from the West is often dependent on fulfillment of good governance and human rights clauses, which the political leaders in Africa find unpalatable and describe as "neo-colonialism," an approach aimed at imposing Western political values on them. China has so far tended to ignore the global lending standards designed to fight corruption in the region. Even the International Monetary Fund and World Bank see their years of painstaking efforts to arrange conditional debt relief being undermined by China's unrestricted lending. But China has elevated "non-interference in other states' internal affairs" as a central tenet of its foreign policy. This has as much to do with making China an attractive partner for the Africans, and also with China's own sensitivities towards outside interference in its own domestic politics. Even as the International Monetary Fund was negotiating structural reforms with the Angolan government in 2004, China stepped in and offered Angola aid without any preconditions, thereby luring Angola away from much needed reforms.

China has also provided modest military assistance to certain regimes in Africa. It is the leading military supplier to Zimbabwe even as Robert Mugabe has used this military hardware and training mainly to contain growing domestic opposition against his government. Mugabe's "Look East" policy, initiated a few years back in response to his regime's ostracism by Western governments for his human rights abuses, has had its biggest success in attracting China to Zimbabwe, so much so that China is now Zimbabwe's second-largest trading partner. China has also supplied arms to both Ethiopia and Eritrea as the two fought each other and faced civil wars. More significant, especially in the light of developments in Darfur, China has a military relationship with the Sudanese government, and despite the United Nations arms embargo, China's military engagement with Sudan has remained close.

China has also started to market its space technology to interested countries in Africa and elsewhere. China has launched a communications satellite for Nigeria, helping not only in designing and building it but also providing a loan to help Nigeria foot the bill. Given Nigeria's reputation as a risky customer, Western companies were reluctant to do business with it and this vacuum was promptly filled by China, allowing it to strengthen its ties with a major oil producer by helping it achieve a greater presence in space.[11] China's "soft" power is also on the ascendant in Africa. China is increasingly being viewed as a land of opportunity and prosperity, replacing the US and Europe in that role in the consciousness of the people of Africa. African students are going to China in larger numbers than ever before. China is leveraging its "soft" power — culture, investment, academia, foreign aid, public diplomacy — more effectively than before to influence Africa and other parts of the developing world.[12]

The Blowback Effect: China Reaps the Whirlwind

While Chinese officials have defended their outreach to Africa, arguing that their support to African nations actually supports a fundamental human right in Africa, the right to development, the question remains whether the Chinese strategy is actually retarding the long-term development of an already impoverished continent. The Chinese policy of extracting natural resources and raw materials from Africa and selling finished manufactured products back is essentially mercantilist in nature and could prove deleterious for the region as a whole. While a boom in China–Africa trade, along with cancellation of debt and aid to

African states, has proved to be mutually advantageous for China and African elites, it has been observed that the long-term political and economic consequences of China's increased involvement in Africa are likely to be deleterious.[13]

The former President of the World Bank, Paul Wolfowitz, has openly criticized Chinese aid policies towards Africa, underscoring the point that Beijing should not repeat the mistakes of the US and the West in bank-rolling unsavory regimes for decades.[14] It is felt that while the lending priorities of global financial institutions such as the World Bank and the International Monetary Fund are being reviewed under pressure from the media and human rights organizations so as to make sure that lending benefits the common man as opposed to just filling up the coffers of the political and economic elites, the entry of China into the foreign aid market has made it difficult to enforce reforms in those countries most in need of it.

China's lending banks do not subscribe to the international guidelines, known as the "Equator Principles," which are used to monitor and manage the social and environmental impact of major outside investments. For example, when the World Bank decided to lend money to the Nigerian government to rebuild its railway system on the condition that corrupt practices were effectively tackled, China offered its own unconditional aid to Nigeria, thereby prolonging the problems inherent in the railway infrastructure of the country. This has been termed "rogue aid," development assistance that is "non-democratic in origin and non-transparent in practice," with the effect of stifling "real progress while hurting ordinary citizens."[15] The ruling elites use such aid to further consolidate their power while the majority of the population continues to stagnate and suffer.

Although opposition to China's policies towards Africa by non-African governments and organizations has been part of the global discourse for some time now, more recently it is from within Africa that voices are rising against many of the Chinese policies. Concerns are rising in Africa that China's economic power is strangling African manufacturing while locking up vital resources for years, as the flood of Chinese finished goods to Africa has created a large trade imbalance. Textile mills in various African states including Nigeria and South Africa have closed down under the onslaught of inexpensive Chinese imports, leading to public protests. In a somewhat surprising outburst, former South African President Thabo

Mbeki warned in 2007 that Africa risked becoming an economic colony of China if the growing trade imbalance between the continent and the Asian dragon is not rectified soon.[16] There is growing political opposition in Zambia to Chinese purchases of mining concessions, with some accusing China of plundering their nation's natural resources. A candidate in the 2007 presidential election promised, if elected, to chase out Chinese investors after riots took place at a Chinese-controlled mine to protest poor treatment and poor remuneration. The Chinese President was forced to cancel his trip to Zambia's Copperbelt Province in 2007 due to the threat of public protests against his visit.[17]

A report by Christian Aid suggests that there is a growing popular perception in Zimbabwe that "Chinese bosses are uniquely brutal and exploitative and that the Zambian state's relationship to them was too close." Notwithstanding the willingness of the political leaders to continue accepting Chinese economic largesse, a perception that China's economic influence is having a negative effect on the domestic labor market and local manufacturing is growing in several African nations. In 2006, Gabon even forced a Chinese energy company to stop drilling for oil due to its environmentally unsafe practices. Chinese-run oil facilities have been targeted by rebel forces in Ethiopia and Sudan. There have been a string of attacks on Chinese nationals in Africa in recent times, underlining the tenuous nature of the Chinese presence in the continent. In Sudan, the rebels have explicitly warned China to re-evaluate its support for the Sudanese government as China is perceived to be indirectly funding the Sudanese government's war effort in Darfur because of its massive investments in Sudan's oil industry.[18]

There are signs that China is now taking this growing criticism from Africa seriously. After all, if charming the Africans is central to China's approach to the region, it makes little sense to alienate the region's inhabitants. China has already taken steps to open up its markets to African commodities and is increasingly investing in production capacities, buying copper mines in Zambia and oil blocks in Nigeria. Over 60 percent of Gambia's and a substantial part of Equatorial Guinea's timber production are under Chinese control. China has also vigorously denied that it plans to create an exclusive sphere of influence in Africa.

During their various trips to Africa, Chinese political leaders make it a point to invoke their country's experience with colonialism and to remind the Africans that China is not a colonial power. According to one of the leaders, "China has never imposed its will or unequal practices on other countries and will never do so in the future."[19] To assuage the concerns in Zambia and South Africa, the Chinese President inaugurated an economic co-operation zone in Zambia and made a donation of $2.6 million to help South Africa in job training and poverty alleviation. In an attempt to differentiate itself from the West, China is making sure that it does not close its doors to African products and has signed agreements opening Chinese markets to Africa's agricultural output.

China is working hard to remove the perception that it is just interested in exploiting the resources of Africa and other regions, and is now also eager to be seen as a force for peace and global stability. As a result, it has recently been more actively engaged in international peacekeeping activities, mostly focused on Africa, from Somalia, Chad, and Liberia to southern Sudan.[20] It was China that played a crucial role in persuading the Sudanese government to allow an expanded United Nations presence in the Darfur region, where a government-backed militia has killed thousands of civilians. Beijing was also instrumental in persuading the United Nations Security Council to deploy peacekeepers in Somalia in 2007 to support the embattled government there. China's support for the leaders of Sudan and Zimbabwe has come under intense global scrutiny in recent years as these regimes remain under pressure to improve their poor human rights records.

The decision of the US government to cut ties with Sudan in the mid-1990s pressured Western oil companies to withdraw and opened new opportunities for Chinese investment. Because of Chinese investment in oil extraction since 1995, Sudan today exports around $2 billion worth of crude oil per year. Not surprisingly, half of that goes to China, accounting for about 5 percent of its total oil imports. China also supplies arms to the Sudanese government, which has been accused of using them against the opposition in the civil war. The sanctions imposed by the West on Sudan are unlikely to be effective so long as Beijing continues with its lucrative partnership with Sudan. Despite various attempts by the West pressure China to help persuade the Sudanese government to accept a strong United Nations peacekeeping force in the war-torn region of Darfur, China long refused to do anything substantive.

China's official position has always been that it will support the

United Nations peacekeepers in Darfur only if the Sudanese government agrees to their presence. Since the Sudanese government was itself the culprit in the atrocities being perpetrated in Darfur, of course it did not acquiesce to the Western demand, resulting in a deadlock. Moreover, much to the West's disappointment, during his last visit to Sudan in 2007, the Chinese President called on the international community to respect the sovereignty of Sudan, even as he wrote off debt and provided a $13 million interest-free loan to build a new presidential palace.[21] China's threat of a veto also prevented the Security Council from taking any effective action to halt the genocidal civil war in Darfur that had already cost the lives of around 300,000 people.

Under pressure from human rights groups in the US and Europe, some of whom have suggested that the 2008 Beijing Olympics should have been boycotted to demonstrate opposition to Chinese policies in Sudan, China modified its earlier stance slightly and has even sent a military engineering unit to help strengthen the fragile African Union (AU) peacekeeping force stationed in Darfur since 2004. A 7,000-strong AU force has been stationed in Darfur to monitor a long-ignored ceasefire but has been deemed largely ineffective due to a lack of resources and a mandate that is extremely restrictive. Initially agreeing to the UN's plan to strengthen the overstretched African Union peacekeeping force in Darfur by accepting a 22,000-strong joint UN-AU force, Sudan's President Omar Al-Bashir backed off from his commitment, saying he would only allow a larger African force with technical and logistical support from the UN. He denounced the idea of non-African troops in Darfur, contending that they would be considered as occupiers and neo-colonialists.

The success of the 2008 Beijing Olympics was crucial for China, which viewed the Games as a confirmation of its rising profile in the international system. The Chinese authorities therefore did their best to resist any linkages between the Beijing Olympics and Chinese policy in Darfur. The George W. Bush administration had described the bloodshed in Darfur as "genocide" and asked China to do more to bring pressure on the Sudanese government. Some members of the US House of Representatives even warned China explicitly that the Beijing Olympics might be jeopardized if China did not change its policies vis-à-vis Sudan. This message was also underscored by many European leaders and influential public figures, leading to subtle changes in China's position.[22]

The Chinese government appointed a special envoy to Darfur and underlined China's support for the UN plan to deploy more than 20,000 soldiers.[23] This forced the Sudanese leadership to reconsider its stand on the UN force and it agreed to a joint UN-AU force in Darfur in June 2007, though it continued to insist that a majority of the soldiers be African and the command of the force to remain with the AU.[24] As a result, the UN Security Council finally decided to dispatch a 26,000-member force to Darfur, the largest peacekeeping unit in the world; deployment began at the end of 2007. Though the African Union transferred authority to the new joint peacekeeping force with the United Nations in Darfur in January 2008, this force did not have the strength and the assets needed to improve the situation in any substantive manner. It was not until late 2008 that the peacekeeping force was able to reach its full strength of 26,000 soldiers. China for its part had sent a 315-man force of military engineers to lay groundwork for the full peacekeeping force by building roads, bridges and landing-strips.[25] Yet there was no long-term change in China's policy towards Sudan, and it seems that China's concessions were most likely just a tactical shift with an eye to the 2008 Olympics. China's actions in Sudan have continued to generate controversy. The Sudan sanctions committee of the United Nations Security Council monitoring compliance with a 2005 arms embargo for Darfur reported in 2010 that bullet castings found at sites of attacks in Darfur on peacekeepers from the United Nations and the African Union were from China.[26]

Conclusions

China's involvement in Africa today is being viewed as part of another "scramble for Africa" comparable to the nineteenth-century exploitation of the region's resources by major Western powers. Today China, along with other major global powers such as the US, Britain, France, and India, is seen by many as interested only in the extraction of Africa's natural resources, making the continent once again an arena of strategic and geopolitical competition among the major powers.[27] While there is an expectation that Africa and its inhabitants would benefit from the growing involvement of outside powers as they extract resources and provide funds for development, concerns are rising that such an approach has only fuelled environmental degradation, economic mismanagement, poverty, and corruption.

As the rising influence of China transforms the balance of power in Africa and threatens to marginalize the US and Europe from their privileged positions on the continent, it is bound to face inevitable reaction from the established major powers. China is viewed as a "free-rider" in the international system, taking advantage of the order and stability being maintained by other great powers. These powers want Beijing to prove it is a "responsible stake-holder" in the global order and contribute towards its maintenance.[28] This implies that the pressure on China to conform to Western norms in its policy towards Africa is bound to increase.

Meanwhile, the US decision to create a new Pentagon command covering Africa, the Africa Command (AFRICOM), is as much directed towards countering China's growing influence on the continent as it is to serving US security interests, such as confronting Islamist terrorism emanating from the Horn of Africa. AFRICOM is aimed at promoting security and stability in the continent, and has not only the traditional responsibilities of a combat command, that is, to facilitate or lead US military operations, but also "a broader soft-power mandate aimed at preemptively reducing conflict."[29] The US has also substantively increased, in fact tripled, its direct humanitarian and development aid to Africa in recent years, with a pledge to double that amount to nearly $9 billion by 2010.[30]

Africa's importance to the US has grown significantly in recent times. The US has been importing more oil from Africa than from the Middle East since 2005, and more from the Gulf of Guinea than from Saudi Arabia and Kuwait combined, with Nigeria alone supplying 10–12 percent of US oil imports. According to the National Intelligence Council, the Gulf of Guinea will supply 20–25 percent of total US oil imports by 2020.[31] The US military presence in Africa is aimed at increasing military co-operation with states in North Africa and the Horn of Africa for anti-terrorism purposes, as well as to enhance co-operation with the West African states for oil security. However, the idea of a new military command in Africa continues to face resistance from the African states who are reluctant to see additional US troops in the continent.[32]

Both China and the US will continue to rely on the use of military force to protect their energy security interests and to ensure a steady supply of affordable energy to their respective countries, though it is not clear how effective military force would be in this realm in the long term. It has been suggested that the US and China could be heading for a collision in Africa in the light of growing instability and competition for resources, though the contest is most likely to be in the diplomatic and development arena.[33] Given the rising stakes for China and the US in Africa, it is highly likely that the diplomatic competition between the two will spill over into other domains.

China's desire to project an image of a peace-loving, responsible global actor is increasingly colliding with its pursuit of economic and strategic interests around the world and Africa is no exception. More importantly, China is now realizing that the tag of "great power" does not come without costs. The reaction in several African states against the Chinese economic push is forcing China to make adjustments to its Africa policy. China can no longer expect that its policies in Africa will remain unexamined by other major states, the global media, and by Africans themselves. As China comes under greater scrutiny, it will be forced to re-evaluate its options vis-à-vis Africa. That process may already be underway.

7

China and the EU
A Relationship Adrift

As the global balance of power shifts to the Asia-Pacific with China and India emerging as the two main pillars of the new international order, major global powers are re-evaluating their policies towards these two regional giants. Because of their size, population, and economic and military capabilities, China and India are today being viewed as the emerging superpowers of the new century, forcing other powers to re-evaluate their strategies. The US as usual has been the first to adapt its strategies to the emerging global realities. On the one hand it is trying to craft a stable relationship with China, and on the other it has vigorously courted India in recent years to such an extent that it has made a major exception for India in the global nuclear non-proliferation order.

The European Union (EU), due to inherent political limitations, has been slow in responding to the new realities. But recently EU has been focusing on China while also taking India more seriously than before. This chapter examines the trends in China's relations with the EU, focusing on the implications of recent EU policy initiatives and their limitations. First, recent trends in EU's ties with China are examined. Subsequently, the constraints on the emerging relationship between the EU and China are analyzed. The chapter concludes with some observations about the future trajectory of the EU's approach towards the changing balance of power.

The EU's Outreach

Since the end of the Cold War, both the EU and China have focused on strengthening their institutional foundations: political in the case of the EU, and economic in the case of China. As the EU became more confident of its economic power and political strength, it has pursued a more outward-oriented foreign policy, and China has been one of the main targets, given China's growing economic weight in the global hierarchy. The EU's China policy has remained focused on improving bilateral cooperation and has emphasized the significance of maintaining a partnership that is strategic in nature. Given the EU's emphasis on multilateral frameworks and China's advocacy of a multipolar world, the EU has found it important to engage China on a whole range of issues with a view to incorporate China into the global institutional order. It is also significant that after the reversion of Hong Kong and Macau to China in 1997 and 1999 respectively, there are no major bilateral irritants in the EU–China relationship.

The EU's approach to China was reflected in the comments of Sir Leon Brittain, the former vice president of the European Commission: "There is no alternative to engagement with China. Indeed the only way in which imaginative and workable solutions will be found is if we recognize that the issues surrounding China's development are global issues which impact directly on our own vital interests. By engaging with China, we are not only in a position to point China towards a path of sustainable growth but we will also be protecting the welfare of Europe into the next millennium and beyond."[1]

The EU's China policy revolves around four pillars: (1) to engage China through an upgraded political dialogue both bilaterally and on the world stage; (2) to help in China's emergence as an open society based upon the rule of law and respect for human rights; (3) to encourage China's complete integration into the global economy and supporting economic and social reforms undergoing in China; and (4) to raise the EU's profile in China.[2]

There has been a significant and consistent movement on all these fronts in the last few years. Annual summits at the heads of government level were initiated in 1998 and since then they have been instrumental in strengthening the dialogue between the EU and China on a range of issues that include human rights, legal cooperation, rural governance, and tourism. The EU and China have also launched negotiations on a new Partnership and Co-operation Agreement which will encompass the full scope of their bilateral relationship, including enhanced co-operation in political matters. These negotiations have updated the 1985 EEC-China Trade and Economic Co-operation Agreement, and will be administered in a relatively independent manner, taking into consideration the global objectives of the EU–China strategic partnership.[3]

Economic and trade ties between the two sides have also been flourishing: China is now the EU's second largest trading partner after the US, and the EU is China's largest trade partner. The overall bilateral trade between the EU and China grew to around 296 billion euros in 2009 and 35 billion euros in services in 2008, with exports from the EU to China growing by approximately 60 percent between 2005 and 2009.[4] In 2010, Europe overtook the US as China's largest trading partner. China's foreign direct investment in Europe, though still small compared with its investments in other regions, has been growing quickly over the last few years.

China's accession to the World Trade Organization (WTO) in 2001 was supported by the EU even though concerns remain about China's implementation of its terms of accession in a timely manner. The EU supported China's entry into the WTO partly because it was concerned about the growing trade deficit in favor of China and had hoped that WTO membership would lead China to lower its trade barriers.[5] While China's entry into the WTO has certainly facilitated an expansion of EU–China bilateral trade, the EU remains far from pleased with China's response. The EU's bilateral trade deficit with China continues to be very large, standing at approximately 128 billion euros in 2009, the EU's largest bilateral trade deficit.

The EU still faces several obstacles to market access in China, including discriminatory licensing procedures, restrictive foreign exchange regulations, lack of protection of Intellectual Property Rights (IPR), and various forms of price controls. The EU intends to help China in further trade and investment liberalization and has initiated sectoral dialogues in key economic areas as well as an EU–China cooperation program that aims to support China's socio-economic transition and its further integration into the global economy. Three areas identified by the EU for cooperation with China in the country strategy paper (CSP) for 2002–2006 are:

- Supporting social and economic reform processes to ensure sustainable economic development and success in the fight against poverty, and China's integration in the world economy, with special emphasis on WTO implementation;
- Aiding in the prevention of environmental degradation and supporting policies that provide a balance between environ-

mental protection and social development in the context of rapid economic growth; and

- Supporting the transition of China to an open society based on the rule of law and respect for human rights.[6]

Several bilateral agreements between the EU and China underpin the cooperative partnership between the two. These include the 1985 EEC–China Trade and Cooperation agreement, the exchange of letters establishing a broad EU–China political dialogue in 1994 and 2002, the 2001 agreement granting Approved Destination Status to China, and the 2000 Science and Technology Agreement.

The interests of the EU and China converge on a range of issues of global import. They are both interested in strengthening multilateral institutions and making them more effective in countering global challenges such as climate change, international terrorism, illegal migration, and global health problems. China's continuing economic stability remains a major concern of EU as China has emerged as the locomotive for regional and global growth. China has been asserting its increasing global power and the EU has been largely supportive of China's pro-active foreign policy. The EU has an interest in making sure that China's rise in Asia and beyond takes place without any disruptive fall-out, as has historically taken place when major powers have risen in the global order. As a result, the EU has been holding regular dialogues with China on issues ranging from human rights, Myanmar, and the Korean Peninsula to Hong Kong and Macau. The EU has also been investing significantly more in the ASEM (Asia-Europe Meeting) process as well as exploring possibilities with the Association of South East Asian Nations (ASEAN) Regional Forum (ARF) as a means to enhance cooperation on international and regional security issues. The EU would like China to further increase its global profile in order to address the insecurities that underlie global tensions and has welcomed China's increasingly active role in the Asia-Pacific. For its part, China perceives the EU as an important actor that should be courted for economic reasons though not nearly as important as the United States. While China recognizes the growing importance of the EU as an economic entity, it does not take the EU seriously as a political unit. Beijing considers getting close to the US a much more important foreign policy priority and it is on this goal that it has focused its diplomatic energies in recent times.

The EU is working hard to raise its visibility in China by

improving internal EU policy cohesion as well as by promoting people-to-people contacts. The similarities between the EU and the Chinese visions of the new global order are being highlighted, and education and cultural exchanges are being intensified though clearly much more remains to be done. The EU views China as a stakeholder in an evolving international system as they both together try to manage the risks and maximize the opportunities presented by the forces of globalization. This makes the EU a stakeholder in China's continued economic success. The EU hopes that by continuing to open up its own economy and by taking a positive lead in addressing common global challenges, China and the EU can work together towards a more stable international political and economic system.

Despite the well-intentioned attempts by EU to engage China more productively in recent years, there are significant constraints that might prevent this relationship from reaching its full potential. This is especially true where differences in political structures and value systems between China and the EU may become more prominent in the future.

Limits to the EU–China Partnership

One of the central tenets of EU policy towards China is to support China's transition towards a more open and plural society that respects fundamental rights and freedoms, protects minorities, and guarantees the rule of law. For the EU, democracy, human rights, and the promotion of liberal political, economic, and social values is of central importance in its bilateral ties with China. And it is here that the limits of the EU–China partnership become apparent. The EU realizes that not withstanding Chinese rhetoric, the present political establishment in China has little or no interest in moving towards greater political openness or towards greater protection of human rights. The evolution of the EU into a post-modern entity shaped by liberal political beliefs and its past experiences collides with the present-day China whose rising economic profile has given it significant leverage to resist any outside attempt to intervene in what it considers its purely domestic terrain.

Even as China decries American hegemony, its leaders have no intention of taking over the American role of the world's policeman anytime soon. However, while declaring that it will focus on internal socio-economic development for the next decade or so, China has actively pursued its interests in a hard-headed fashion, even actively working to prevent the rise of other regional powers, or at least to limit their development relative to itself. On the other hand, public opinion in Europe makes it difficult for the EU to ignore the issues of human rights and political values. While publicly both sides have tried to play down their disputes over human rights, the Chinese government has increasingly found it difficult to rebut its critics in the West who have pointed to China's increasing restrictions on media and decreasing political tolerance in recent times.[7]

It is in this context that the issue of Taiwan and Tibet assumes significance. For Beijing, the issue of Taiwan is of utmost importance and Taiwan's reunification with mainland China is one of its top priorities. There are a range of views on Taiwan among the EU member states, though its official position is that the EU supports a peaceful resolution between China and Taiwan and follows a one-China policy. In the policy paper on the EU that China published in 2003, it made it clear that proper handling of the Taiwan question is essential to a steady growth of China–EU relations. China would like EU exchanges with Taiwan to be strictly unofficial and non-governmental. Similarly, on the issue of Tibet the policy paper asks the EU not to have any contact with the "Tibetan government in exile" and not to provide facilities to the supporters of Dalai Lama.[8] And China tries its best to make sure that the EU gets this message. When the French President, Nocolas Sarkozy, decided to meet the Dalai Lama in 2008, China went ahead and cancelled the EU–China annual summit.

More recently, China has started asserting itself in the UN, but not in a manner that the EU was perhaps hoping for. China's tacit support for the genocidal regime in Sudan forced the EU to take a more hard-line position in favor of external intervention in Darfur. But China's veto in the UN Security Council continues to prevent any meaningful action being taken by the UN on this issue. China's active collaboration, including military, with regimes in Iran, Myanmar, Zimbabwe, Liberia, and Chad has also put the issue of values at the forefront of EU–China relations.

The EU's arms embargo on China is another major irritant in this relationship. While the EU has indicated that it is working towards lifting the embargo, it has not specified a final timetable as to when this might happen. This issue will continue to haunt EU–China ties because the EU will have to take into account the concerns of the US before making any final decision. Similarly, China is frustrated with EU for not granting its economy Market Economy Status. The EU continues to insist that China does not yet meet the criteria set out by the European Commission for countries to be granted that status. China's growing economic competitiveness has been a topic of intense debate among EU member nations. Pressure is also building in the EU for taking a more aggressive stance on the lack of protection of intellectual property rights in China. While the EU has adopted a relatively low-key approach to this issue compared with the US, that policy may change in the near future. The EU has joined the US and Canada in taking the case of China's tariffs on auto parts to the WTO.

The EU's fast growing trade deficit with China and the EU's trade barriers will continue to cause friction between the two, despite a booming trade relationship. It is the southern European countries that are most affected by Chinese imports, and they have started putting pressure on the EU to harden its position on China-related trade and economic policies. The EU has repeatedly asked China to lower trade barriers to foreign firms and raise low labor and environmental standards that have helped boost China's export might. It has expressed concerns about restrictions that European companies face in doing business in China that range from rules that force foreign companies into joint ventures with Chinese partners to rampant counterfeiting, closed public procurement markets, and discriminatory regulations.[9] This pressure is expected to increase, and avoiding economic clashes will be a critical task for both China and the EU.China is trying to emerge as a major partner of European nations hit hard by the 2008 global financial crisis and in so doing trying to gain greater influence over the economic policies set in Brussels. Beijing hopes that by investing in Europe it will be able to garner European support for its position on divisive currency issues and in trade disputes at the World Trade Organization.[10] However, the growing Chinese presence in Europe will cause friction with established economic players. When China outbid European companies to build a highway in Poland in 2009 with European subsidies, German Chancellor, Angela Merkel, was forced to publicly call for reciprocity.[11] These tensions are only likely to grow in the future.

While both China and the EU may prefer a multipolar world order as opposed to an order dominated by the United States, they have different long-term priorities. China increasingly views itself as a superpower-in-waiting and would like to compete with the United States for global supremacy. China would like the EU to play the role of a counterweight to the United States in this struggle. The EU on the other hand would like a world order where hard power matters less and less, and where effective global governance is provided by international institutions such as the United Nations and the WTO.[12] Moreover, the EU is the closest ally of the United States and despite some recent strains in the trans-Atlantic partnership, the EU has greatly benefited from the global preponderance of the United States. While some European states such as France may find the United States overbearing, the EU as a whole has no intention of challenging the United States. Simply put, the EU has neither the capabilities nor any inclination to counter-balance American might. China, on the other hand, is gearing itself up to challenge the United States, and if the EU is forced to make a choice between the current superpower and its challenger, it is not difficult to guess what the EU's choice would be.

Recognizing the limits of the EU–China partnership, the EU has initiated an outreach towards India, the other rising power in Asia, with which it shares some important values. Ties between the EU and India have significantly strengthened in recent years. Though India was among the first countries to establish diplomatic relations with the European Economic Community, it was only recently that the EU formalized its ties with India into a "strategic partnership."[13] The EU and India decided to launch a strategic partnership initiative in 2004. This is very significant, as the EU has strategic partnerships with only five other countries: the US, Canada, Russia, Japan, and China. Under politically favorable conditions, India–EU bilateral relations have progressed from trade and development cooperation during the Cold War to a political dialogue in the 1990s culminating in a comprehensive strategic partnership. Bilateral ties have grown exponentially since 2004, when the leaders of the two blocs decided to hold annual EU–India summits. The aim is to have a much stronger relationship on a variety of issues including political, economic, science and technology, academic, cultural, and civil society.

The EU's gradual gravitation towards India is also the result of a growing unease with China's economic dominance. Not only is India seen as a better enforcer of Intellectual Property Rights (IPR), but diversification also seems to be a better strategy for Europe.

While China is seen as not being fully integrated into the international system, India, being a liberal democracy, is considered as almost a kindred spirit. As the largest open societies in the world, the EU and India share a commitment to participatory democracy, human rights, good governance, and the rule of law.

Despite growing ties of the EU with China and India at the official level, it is the US and the UK that remain the primary point of reference for most ordinary Chinese (and Indians for that matter) as far as "the West" is concerned. It has been rightly observed that "for the great majority of Indians, most of Europe is a strange land, an exotic place for tourism to which only a privileged layer of society had had access."[14] The same, it can safely be assumed, is true for the great majority of Chinese. The complex nature of the EU as an institution also makes it difficult for ordinary people to comprehend the exact role that it plays in politics: Europe continues to be an amalgam of different cultures and identities. In both China and India, the EU suffers because of its low profile and visibility.

Despite claims that there is an emerging coherent EU foreign policy, so far the divergent interests of various EU states have been more influential in shaping the EU's foreign policy in general and its approach towards China in particular. Unless the EU gets its act together as an institution working towards common foreign policy objectives, it will soon recognize that China will also find it difficult to take it seriously and will continue to deal with the EU states on an individual basis.

At the governmental level, the EU should not assume that ignoring difficult issues such as human rights or unfair trade practices will take it very far with China. It should be firm yet principled in dealing with the Middle Kingdom.

The EU should also expand its ties with India faster and more meaningfully than hitherto. India's role as a strategic balancer in the Asia-Pacific is going to be crucial in the coming years, and if the EU decides to ignore India now, it will lose out vis-à-vis the US in gaining sufficient diplomatic leverage in the region.

As the center of gravity shifts to the Asia-Pacific and the international system undergoes a profound re-ordering, the EU is trying hard to adjust to these new global realities. The rise of China and India has presented the EU with several opportunities that it is trying its best to harness. But while trade and economics seems to have given the EU a reference point vis-à-vis the two Asian giants, politically it seems adrift as it is finding it difficult to speak with one voice on the political issues that confront the world today. Europe is finding it difficult to formulate a coherent foreign policy for all of its member nations and this has made it difficult for the EU to respond effectively to the rise of China. The United States has taken the lead in defining its relations with China and the EU now seems to be reluctantly following its lead rather than acting as an autonomous political unit keeping in mind its own strategic priorities. The balance of power between the EU and China has altered so dramatically in recent years that when the European leaders visit China these days, to many they "appear like mendicants before the imperial throne, begging for business to lift their faltering economies."[15]

Moreover, the EU's worldview is, not surprisingly, shaped by its historical experiences and it seems intent on exploiting the opportunities provided by the liberal global economic order. Nonetheless, to think of foreign policy as nothing more than an extension of economic policy, and to consider international politics as nothing but the sum of global trade and economic cooperation, is a liberal fallacy which assumes that if only nations would trade with each other more, the world would become more prosperous and peaceful. The problem with these assumptions is that not only is there little empirical evidence to indicate that more trade leads to peace and tranquility, but further, while politics and economics are certainly interrelated, the international economic system depends upon the international political order and not vice versa. The EU's lack of a strategic direction in foreign policy makes it difficult for it to respond effectively to new challenges such as the rise of China.

The good news, however, is that the EU has now started engaging China seriously, and despite some inherent limits in this relationships, there is no reason why China and the EU cannot cultivate a long-term sustainable partnership. But the EU will have to move beyond trade and economics to give this relationship greater meaning and substance. Otherwise there is a danger that China's rise and America's relative decline might further marginalize Europe in global affairs.

Notes

1 Introduction

1 "China Plans to Slow Expansion of Defense Spending in 2010," *Washington Post*, March 5, 2010.

2 Shen Dingli, "Don't Shun the Idea of Setting up Military Bases Overseas," January 28, 2010, available at http://www.china.org.cn/opinion/2010-01/28/content_19324522.htm

3 John J. Mearsheimer, *The Tragedy of Great Power Politics* (New York: W.W. Norton, 2001), p. 42.

4 For a theoretical account of hegemonic transitions, see Robert Gilpin, *War and Change in Global Politics* (Cambridge: Cambridge University Press, 1981).

5 Keith Bradsher, "China Still Band Rare Earth to Japan," *New York Times*, November 10, 2010.

6 Fareed Zakaria, "President Obama, Asia is calling," *Washington Post*, November 2, 2010.

7 "Fear of the Dragon," *The Economist*, January 11, 2010.

8 Robert Fogel, "$123,000,000,000,000," *Foreign Policy*, January/February 2010.

9 For the seminal exposition of the reasons behind the rise and subsequent decline of great powers, see Paul Kennedy, *The Rise and Fall of the Great Powers: Economic Change and Military Conflict from 1500 to 2000* (New York: Random House, 1987).

10 This argument is made in detail in Michael D. Swaine and Ashley J. Tellis, *Interpreting China's Grand Strategy: Past, Present and Future* (Santa Monica, CA: Rand Corp., 2000).

11 Raphael Israeli, "The People's Republic of China and the PLO," in Augustus Richard Norton and Martin Greenberg, eds., *The International Relations of the Palestine Liberation Organization* (Carbondale, IL: Southern Illinois University Press, 1989).

12 Alan Hutchinson, *China's Africa Revolution* (London: Hutchinson & Co, 1975).

13 On "soft balancing" see Robert A. Pape, "Soft Balancing Against the United States," *International Security* 30.1 (Summer 2005), pages 7–45.

14 On China's use of "soft power" see Joshua Kurlantzick, *Charm*

Offensive: How China's Soft Power is Transforming the World (New Haven, CT: Yale University Press, 2007).

15 See the US Department of Defense's 2010 Report to the Congress on Military and Security Developments Involving the People's Republic of China, available at http://www.defense.gov/pubs/pdfs/2010_CMPR_Final.pdf

16 Greg Toorde, "How the US Ambushed China in its Backyard," *South China Morning Post*, July 25, 2010.

17 Thomas Wright, "How China Gambit Backfired," *The Diplomat*, July 28, 2010.

18 Evan A. Feigenbaum, China's Rise and the Contested Commons, *Council on Foreign Relations*, August 18, 2010.

19 Dan Blumenthal, "Reining in China's Ambitions," *Wall Street Journal*, July 26, 2010.

20 For details, see the US Department of Defense's 2010 Report to the Congress on Military and Security Developments Involving the People's Republic of China.

21 Mark Landler and Sewell Chan, "Taking Harder Stance Toward China, Obama Lines Up Allies," *New York Times*, October 2, 2010.

22 Andrew Higgins, "As China finds bigger place in world affairs, its wealth breeds hostility," *Washington Post*, September 8, 2010.

2 China in the Asia-Pacific

1 See Aaron Friedberg, "Will Europe's Past Be Asia's Future?" *Survival* 42.3 (Autumn, 2000), pp. 147–159.

2 For a discussion of the various interpretations of China's "peaceful rise," see Evan S. Medeiros, "China Debates Its 'Peaceful Rise' Strategy?" available at http://yaleglobal.yale.edu/display. article? id=4118.

3 On why multipolar systems are less stable than bipolar ones, see Kenneth Waltz, *Theory of International Politics*. Also see John Mearsheimer, *Tragedy of Great Power Politics* (New York: W.W. Norton, 2001), pp. 138–167.

4 A detailed explication of the Power Transition Theory can be found in A.F.K. Organski and Jacek Kugler, *The War Ledger* (Chicago: University of Chicago Press, 1980).

5 For an assessment of the great power potential of China, India, and Japan in the 1980s, see Stephen Cohen, "Toward a Great State in Asia?" in Onkar Marwah and Jonathan D. Pollack (eds.), *Military Power and Policy in Asian States: China, India, and Japan* (Boulder, CO: Westview, 1980), pp. 9–41.

6 Bill Emmott, *Rivals: How the Power Struggle Between China, India and Japan Will Shape Our Next Decade* (London: Allen Lane, 2008), pp. 1–24.

7 John Pomfret, "US Sells Weapons to Taiwan, Angering China," *Washington Post*, January 30, 2010.

8 Stanley W. Weiss, "Rowing Between Two Reefs," *New York Times*, August 30, 2010.

9 "China could attack India before 2012, claims analyst," *Press Trust of India*, July 12, 2009.

10 On the present state of Sino-Indian relations, see Harsh V. Pant, *The China Syndrome: Grappling With an Uneasy Relationship* (New Delhi: HarperCollins, 2010).

11 Condoleezza Rice, "Promoting the National Interest," *Foreign Affairs* 79.1 (January/February 2000), p. 56.

12 The 2006 Quadrennial Defense Review Report is available at http://www.defenselink.mil/qdr/report/Report20060203.pdf.

13 Ashley Tellis, "India in Asian Geopolitics," in Prakash Nanda (ed.), *Rising India: Friends and Foes* (New Delhi: Lancer Publishers, 2007), pp. 123–127.

14 On the role of nationalism in the shaping of Japan–China ties see Yutaka Kawashima, *Japanese Foreign Policy at the Crossroads* (Washington, DC: Brookings Institution Press, 2003), pp. 104–106.

15 Robert Marquand, "Anti-Japan Protests Jar an Uneasy Asia," *The Christian Science Monitor*, April 11, 2005.

16 Martin Fackler and Ian Johnson, "Arrest in Disputed Sea Riles China and Japan," *New York Times*, September 19, 2010.

17 S.D. Naik, "India–Japan Ties — Moving to the Next Level," *The Hindu Business Line*, January 2, 2007.

18 Tukoji R. Pandit, "Sun Shines on India–Japan Relations," *The Asian Tribune*, December 29, 2006.

3   China in South Asia

1 C. Raja Mohan, "Beyond India's Monroe Doctrine," *The Hindu*, January 2, 2003.

2 Asif Ali Zardari, "Sino-Pakistan Relations Higher than Himalayas," *China Daily*, February 23, 2009.

3 James Martin Center for Nonproliferation Studies, "Pakistan Profile," published on the website Nuclear Threat Initiative, January 2009, available at http://www.nti.org/e_research/profiles/Pakistan/index.html.

4 Ananth Krishnan, "China's Fighter Jets for Pakistan," *The Hindu*, November 11, 2009.

5 C. Raja Mohan, "Dragon in Space," *Indian Express*, April 24, 2007.

6 Gordon C. Chang, "Iran Tried to Buy the Pakistani Bomb. What was China's Role?" *Fox Forum*, March 17, 2010.

7 R. Jeffry Smith and Joby Warrick, "A Nuclear Power's Act of Proliferation," *Washington Post*, November 13, 2009.

8 John W. Garver, *Protracted Contest: Sino-Indian Rivalry in the Twentieth Century* (Seattle: University of Washington Press, 2001), p. 188.

9 For an argument along similar lines, see Stephen P. Cohen, "Geostrategic Factors in India–Pak Relations," *Asian Affairs*, Vol. 10, No. 3 (Fall 1983): 24–31, 28.

10 Ziad Haider, "The China Factor in Pakistan," *Far Eastern Economic Review*, October 2, 2009.

11 "Pak Now Hands China a 'Blank Cheque', India Says No Way," *Indian Express*, February 23, 2010.

12 For details see Gordon G. Chang, "India's China Problem," *Forbes*, August 13, 2009.

13 Saibal Dasgupta, "Arms Sale to Pak Justified as India Buys from US: Chinese Official," *Times of India*, December 22, 2008.

14 "Chinese Media Sees Red," *Press Trust of India*, March 3, 2006.

15 Farhan Bokhari, "Pakistan in Talks To Buy Chinese Reactors," *Financial Times*, January 2, 2006.

16 Mark Hibbs, "Pakistan Deal Signals China's Growing Nuclear Assertiveness," Nuclear Energy Brief, Carnegie Endowment for International Peace, April 27, 2010.

17 Ziad Haider, "Oil Fuels Beijing's New Power Game," *Yale Global Online*, available at http://yaleglobal.yale.edu/display.article?id=5411.

18 Saibal Dasgupta, "China Mulls Setting Up Military Base in Pakistan," *Times of India*, January 28, 2010.

19 *Annual Report: 2008–2009*, Ministry of Defence, Government of India, p. 6.

20 "China's Positioning on the Border is Very Aggressive," *India Abroad*, April 3, 2010.

21 For details, see the joint statement by President Barack Obama and President Hu Jintao, November 17, 2009, available at http://www.whitehouse.gov/the-press-office/joint-press-statement-president-obama-and-president-hu-china.

22 S.M. Burke, *Pakistan's Foreign Policy* (London: Oxford University Press, 1973), p. 213.

23 Kathryn Jacques, *Bangladesh, India, and Pakistan: International Relations and Regional Tensions in South Asia* (New York: St. Martin's Press, 2000), p. 161.

24 Pranab Dhal Samanta, "Breaking 10-Year Silence, China Reveals It's No 1 Arms Supplier to Bangladesh," *Indian Express*, September 9, 2007.

25 Sumit Sen, "Bangladesh Building Missile Arsenal," *Times of India*, September 12, 2008.

26 Tarique Niazi, "China's March on South Asia," *China Brief*, Vol. 5, No. 9, April 26, 2005.

27 Ramtanu Maitra, "Prospects Brighten for Kunming Initiative," *Asia Times Online*, February 12, 2003, http://www.atimes.com/ atimes/ South_Asia/EB12Df04.html.

28 *The Assam Tribune*, March 23, 2010.

29 Vijay Sakhuja, "China–Bangladesh Relations and Potential for Regional Tensions," *China Brief*, July 23, 2009.

30 J.N. Dixit, *Liberation and Beyond: Indo-Bangladesh Relations* (New Delhi: Konark, 1999), p. 283.

31 "Hasina Meets Wen To Deepen 'Comprehensive Partnership'," *Press Trust of India*, March 18, 2010.

32 "Who is Greater Friend? India or China? Dhaka Debates," *Indo-Asian News Service*, March 19, 2010.

33 Dhirendra Mohan Prasad, *Ceylon's Foreign Policy under the Bandarnaikes (1956–65): A Political Analysis* (New Delhi: S. Chand, 1973), pp. 304–388.

34 Garver, *Protracted Contest*, pp. 308–309.

35 For a detailed examination of this accord, see Shelton U. Kodikara, "Genesis of the Indo-Sri Lankan Agreement of 29 July, 1987," *Contemporary South Asia*, Vol. 4, No. 2 (July 1995), pp. 171–185.

36 For a discussion of the factors responsible for the defeat of the LTTE, see Harsh V. Pant, "End Game in Sri Lanka," *Yale Global Online*, February 23, 2009, available at http://yaleglobal.yale.edu/content/end-game-sri-lanka.

37 Ibid.

38 Sutirtho Patranobis, "China Creates a Pearl in Sri Lanka," *Hindustan Times*, September 16, 2009.

39 Ashok K. Mehta, "Colombo Looks Beyond Delhi," *The Pioneer*, March 18, 2009.

40 "Come to Us for Weapons: Narayanan to Lanka," *Indian Express*, June 1, 2007.

41 This and other geographical details regarding Nepal can be found at the Central Intelligence Agency's World Factbook, available at https://www.cia.gov/library/publications/the-world-factbook/geos/ np.html.

42 For a detailed discussion on Tibet's strategic importance for China, see Rama Kant, "Nepal's China Policy," *China Report*, Vol. 30, No. 2, pp. 164–166.

43 Narayan Khadka, "Chinese Foreign Policy Towards Nepal in Cold War Period: An Assessment," *China Report*, Vol. 35, No. 1, pp. 62–65.

44 Garver, *Protracted Contest*, p. 140.

45 The full text of the 1950 Treaty of Peace and Friendship is available at http://meadev.nic.in/economyibta/volume1/chapter38.htm.

46 For details on the Indian economic blockade of Nepal, see Garver, *Protracted Contest*, pp. 155–162.

47 "Nepal for Equidistant Ties with India, China," *India Abroad*, June 23, 2008.

48 For an example of how smaller South Asian states have used China as a leverage in their dealings with India, see Manish Dabhade and Harsh V. Pant, "Coping with Challenges to Sovereignty: Sino-Indian Rivalry and Nepal's Foreign Policy," *Contemporary South Asia*, Vol. 13, No. 2 (June 2004), pp. 157–169.

49 Harsh V. Pant, "India's China Policy: Devoid of a Strategic Framework," *South Asian Survey*, Vol. 12, No. 2, pp. 210–217.

4   China in the Indian Ocean

1 For details, see https://www.cia.gov/library/publications/the-world-factbook/geos/xo.html.

2 P.K. Das, "Maritime Dimensions of India's Security," *Indian Defence Review*, Vol. 18, No. 2 (2003), pp. 43–47.

3 Petter Stålenheim, Catalina Perdomo and Elisabeth Sköns, "Military Expenditure," in *SIPRI Year Book 2007: Armaments, Disarmament and International Security* (London: Oxford University Press, 2007), pp. 289–290.

4 Ibid.

5 Anthony H. Cordesman and Martin Kleiber, *The Asian Conventional Military Balance in 2006*, published online by The Center for Strategic and International Studies, Washington DC, June 2006, p. 32, at http://csis.org/files/media/csis/pubs/060626_asia_balance_powers .pdf.

6 Robert D. Kaplan, "Lost at Sea," *New York Times*, September 21, 2007.

7 *The Military Balance 2008* (London: The International Institute for Strategic Studies, 2008), pp. 360–61.

8 Thomas Kane, *Chinese Grand Strategy and Maritime Power* (London: Frank Cass, 2002), p. 139.

9 Youssef Bodansky, "The PRC Surge for the Strait of Malacca and Spratly Confronts India and the US," Defense and Foreign Affairs Strategic Policy, Washington, DC, September 30, 1995, pp. 6–13.

10 Manu Pubby, "China's New N-Submarine Base Sets Off Alarm Bells," *Indian Express*, May 3, 2008.

11 Bill Gertz, "China Builds Up Strategic Sea Lanes," *Washington Times*, January 18, 2005.

12 For a detailed explication the security ramifications of the Chinese "string of pearls" strategy, see Gurpreet Khurana, "China's 'String of Pearls' in the Indian Ocean and Its Security Implications," *Strategic Analysis*, Vol. 32, No. 1 (January 2008), pp. 1–22.

13 For a nuanced analysis of this, see Andrew Selth, "Chinese Military Bases in Burma: The Explosion of a Myth," Griffith Asia Institute, Regional Outlook Paper No. 10, 2007.

14 Ziad Haider, "Oil Fuels Beijing's New Power Game," *Yale Global Online*, March 11, 2005, available at http://yaleglobal.yale.edu/display. article?id=5411.

15 Geoffrey Till, *Seapower: A Guide for the Twenty-First Century* (London: Frank Cass, 2004), p. 102.

16 Harsh V. Pant, "India in the Asia-Pacific: Rising Ambitions with an Eye on China," *Asia-Pacific Review*, Vol. 14, No. 1 (May, 2007), pp. 54–71.

17 Manu Pubby, "Indian Submarine, Chinese Warship Test Each Other in Pirate Waters," *Indian Express*, February 5, 2009.

18 *Indian Maritime Doctrine*, Integrated Headquarters, Ministry of Defence (Navy), 2004, p. 56.

19 Rahul Roy-Chaudhury, *Sea Power and India's Security* (London: Brassey's, 1995), p. 199.

20 K.M. Pannikar, *India and the Indian Ocean: An Essay in the Influence of Sea Power on Indian History* (London: George Allen & Unwin, 1945), p. 45.

21 David Scott, "India's 'Grand Strategy' for the Indian Ocean: Mahanian Visions," *Asia-Pacific Review*, Vol. 13, No. 2 (2006), pp. 98–101.

22 George Tanham, *Securing India* (New Delhi: Manohar Publishers, 1996), p. 59.

23 N. Palmer, "South Asia and the Indian Ocean," in A. Cottrell and R. Burrell (eds.), *The Indian Ocean: Its Political, Economic, and Military Importance* (New York: Praeger, 1972), p. 237.

24 Ashley Tellis, "Demanding Tasks for the Indian Navy," *Asian Survey*, Vol. 25, No. 12 (December, 1985), p. 1204.

25 Quoted in Gavin Rabinowitz, "India, China Jostle for Influence in Indian Ocean," *The Associated Press*, June 7, 2008.

26 E. Margolis, "India Rules the Waves," *US Naval Institute Proceedings*, Vol. 131, No. 3 (March, 2005), p. 70.

27 Sam J. Tangredi, "The Future of Maritime Power," in Andrew T.H. Tan (ed.), *The Politics of Maritime Power: A Survey* (London: Routledge, 2007), pp. 143–44.

28 *Freedom to Use the Seas: India's Maritime Military Strategy*, Integrated Headquarters Ministry of Defence (Navy), 2007, p. 41.

29 On recent trends in US–India ties, see Harsh V. Pant, *Contemporary Debates in Indian Foreign and Security Policy: India Negotiates Its Rise in the International System* (New York: Palgrave Macmillan, 2008), pp. 19–38.

30 Colin Powell, "US Looks to its Allies for Stability in Asia and the Pacific," *International Herald Tribune*, January 27, 2001.

31 "United States: New Naval Strategy," *International Herald Tribune*, October 25, 2007.

32 Sandeep Dikshit, "Join Global Policing of Sea Lanes, US Asks India," *The Hindu*, April 19, 2007.

33 On India–Japan maritime cooperation, see Gurpreet Khurana, "Security of Sea-Lanes: Prospects for India–Japan Cooperation," *Strategic Analysis*, Vol. 31, No. 1 (January, 2007), pp. 139–150.

34 On India's strategic priorities in the Asia-Pacific, see Pant, "India in the Asia-Pacific: Rising Ambitions with an Eye on China," *Asia-Pacific Review*, Vol. 14, No. 1 (May, 2007), pp. 54–71.

35 Yevgeny Bendersky et al., "India's Project Seabird and the Indian Ocean's Balance of Power," *Power and Interest News Report*, July 20, 2005.

36 Mohan Malik, "Chinese Strategy of Containing India," *Power and Interest News Report*, February 6, 2006.

37 Pranab Dhal Samanta, "Start Getting Used to DSP: Defence Services Provider," *Indian Express*, January 1, 2008.

38 Manu Pubby, "3rd Aircraft Carrier to be Inducted by 2017: Antony," *Indian Express*, May 17, 2007.

39 Sandeep Unnithan, "Battle Over Gorshkov," *India Today*, December 7, 2007.

40 See Stephen Cohen's interview with Pragati is available at http://pragati.nationalinterest.in/wp-content/uploads/2008/06/pragati-issue15-jun2008-communityed.pdf.

41 John W. Garver, *Protracted Contest: Sino-Indian Rivalry in the Twentieth Century* (Seattle: University of Washington Press, 1989), p. 285.

5   China in the Middle East

1 For a full explication of this argument, see Michael D. Swaine and Ashley J. Tellis, *Interpreting China's Grand Strategy: Past, Present and Future* (Santa Monica, CA: Rand Corp., 2000).

2 Matthew Forney, "China's Quest for Oil," *Time Magazine*, October 18, 2004, http://www.time.com/time/magazine/article/0,9171,501041025-725174,00.html.

3 S. Henderson, *China and Oil: The Middle East Dimension*, The Washington Institute for Near East Policy, September 2004, http://www.thewashingtoninstitute.org/templateC05.php?CID=1776.

4 *SIPRI Yearbook 2007: Armaments, Disarmament and International Security* (Oxford: Oxford University Press, 2007), pp. 288–90.

5 For the period 2002 to 2006 the Stockholm International Peace Research Institute (SIPRI) ranked China as the world's largest weapons importer, importing over $14 billion worth of conventional weapons (ibid., p. 418).

6 Harsh V. Pant, *Contemporary Debates in Indian Foreign and Security Policy: India Negotiates Its Rise in the International System* (New York: Palgrave Macmillan, 2008), pp. 165–67.

7 Harsh V. Pant, "Saudi Arabia Woos China and India," *Middle East Quarterly*, Vol. 13, No. 4 (Fall, 2006), pp. 45–52, available at http://www.meforum.org/article/1019.

8 Richard F. Grimmett, "Conventional Arms Transfers to Developing Countries (2002–2009)," Congressional Research Service, September 10, 2010, available at http://www.fas.org/sgp/crs/weapons/R41403. pdf.

9 The former President of China, Jiang Zemin, is supposed to have stated in 1994 that China should oppose "hegemony" by helping dissident countries like Iran. See Jonathan Rynhold and Deng-Ker Lee, "Peking's Middle East Policy in the Post Cold War Era," *Issues and Studies*, Vol. 30, No. 8 (August, 1994), pp. 69–94, at 85.

10 Robin Wright, "Deepening China–Iran Ties Weaken Bid to Isolate Iran," *Washington Post*, November 18, 2007, available at http://www.washingtonpost.com/wp-dyn/content/article/2007/11/17/ AR2007111701680.html.

11 Jin Liangxiang, "Energy First: China and the Middle East," *Middle East Quarterly*, Vol. 12, No. 2 (Spring, 2005), pp. 3–10, available at http://www.meforum.org/article/694.

12 Robert Lowe and Claire Spencer, eds., *Iran, Its Neighbours and the Regional Crises* (Chatham House, 2006), http://www.chathamhouse. org.uk/files/3376_iran0806.pdf.

13 *SIPRI Yearbook 2007*, pp. 409–11.

14 John J. Tkachik, Jr. "Confront China's Support for Iran's Nuclear Weapons," The Heritage Foundation, April 18, 2006, http://www. heritage.org/research/asiaandthepacific/wm1042.cfm.

15 In December 2006 the UN Security Council imposed a series of sanctions on Iran for its non-compliance with an earlier Security Council resolution calling on Iran to immediately suspend enrichment-related activities. These sanctions were primarily targeted against the transfer of nuclear and ballistic missile technologies, and in response to the concerns of China and Russia, were lighter than those sought by the United States.

The scope of the sanctions was widened in March 2007 and they were further extended in March 2008 to cover additional financial institutions, restrict the travel of additional persons, and bar the export of nuclear- and missile-related dual-use goods to Iran. In June 2010, the Security Council approved fresh sanctions against Tehran that included measures prohibiting Iran from buying heavy weapons such as attack helicopters and missiles as well as toughening the rules on financial transactions with Iranian banks and increasing the number of Iranian individuals and companies targeted with asset freezes and travel bans.

16 "The Worldwide Threat: Evolving Dangers in a Complex World,"

testimony of the Director of Central Intelligence, George J. Tenet, before the Senate Select Committee on Intelligence, February 11, 2003, available at http://www.cia.gov/cia/public_affairs/speeches/dci_speech_02112003.html.

17 John Pomfret, "US says Chinese businesses and banks are bypassing UN sanctions against Iran," *Washington Post*, October 18, 2010.

18 "China, Saudi Arabia to Boost Trade," *China Daily*, January 12, 2010.

19 See *China's Global Quest for Energy*, The Institute for the Analysis of Global Security, January 2007, http://fmso.leavenworth.army.mil/documents/chinasquest0107.pdf.

20 Nawaf Obaid, *Saudi Arabia's Strategic Energy Initiative: Safeguarding Against Supply Disruptions*, November 2006, http://www.stimson.org/newcentury/pdf/OilPresCS.pdf.

21 The embargo on weapons sales to China by the European Union and the United States, put in place as a result of the violent suppression of the Tiananmen Square protests, still remains in place today. The PRC has been calling for a lifting of the ban for many years and has had a varying amount of support from members of the Council of the European Union.

22 "New China Defense Paper Heightens Threat vs. Taiwan; Russia, Israel are China's Top Arms Suppliers," *China Reform Monitor*, January 14, 2005, http://www.asianresearch.org/articles/2477.html.

23 Pang Li, "Israel to Enhance Relationship with China," April 26, 2010, available at http://www.china.org.cn/world/2010-04/26/content_19907844.htm.

24 Ibid.

25 Ibid.

26 Le Tian, "China, Arab Nations Sign Action Plan," *China Daily*, June 2, 2006, http://www.chinadaily.com.cn/china/2006-06/02/content_606717.htm.

6   China in Africa

1 For the seminal exposition of the reasons behind the rise and subsequent decline of great powers, see Paul Kennedy, *The Rise and Fall of the Great Powers: Economic Change and Military Conflict from 1500 to 2000* (New York: Random House, 1987).

2 The statistics on China's oil consumption in comparison with other countries are available at http://www.xist.org/charts/en_oilcons.aspx.

3 On "soft balancing" see Robert A. Pape, "Soft Balancing Against the United States," *International Security*, Vol. 30 No. 1 (Summer, 2005), pp. 7–45.

4 The Chinese Government's white paper on Africa released in 2006 is available at http://news.xinhuanet.com/english/2006-01/12/content_4042521.htm.

5 I. Taylor, "Taiwan's Foreign Policy and Africa: The Limitations of Dollar Diplomacy," *Journal of Contemporary China*, Vol. 11, No. 30 (2002), pp. 125–140.

6 For a detailed explication of this argument, see Bruce D. Larkin, *China and Africa, 1949–1970: The Foreign Policy of the People's Republic of China* (Berkeley, CA: University of California Press, 1971).

7 Alan Hutchinson, *China's Africa Revolution* (London: Hutchinson & Co, 1975).

8 "Trade with Africa set to achieve record high," *People's Daily*, October 15, 2010.

9 "Summit Adopts Declaration, Action Plan," *China Daily*, November 5, 2006.

10 David Blair, "Oil-Hungry China Takes Sudan Under Its Wings," *The Telegraph*, April 23, 2005.

11 Jim Yardley, "Snubbed by US, China Finds New Space Partners," *New York Times*, May 24, 2007.

12 On China's recent reliance on its soft power in dealing with other states, see Joshua Kurlantzick, *Charm Offensive: How China's Soft Power is Transforming the World* (New Haven, CT: Yale University Press, 2007).

13 Denis M. Tull, "China's Engagement in Africa: Scope, Significance and Consequences," *Journal of Modern African Studies*, Vol. 44 No. 3 (2006), pp. 459–479.

14 "World Bank President Criticizes China's Banks Over Africa Lending," *International Herald Tribune*, October 23, 2006.

15 Moises Naim, "Help Not Wanted," *New York Times*, February 15, 2007.

16 Yaroslav Trofimov, "In Africa, China's Expansion Begins to Stir Resentment," *Wall Street Journal*, February 2, 2007.

17 Ibid.

18 Mohamed Osman, "Darfur Rebels Attack Oil Field, Warn Chinese to Leave Sudan," *Associated Press*, October 26, 2007.

19 Craig Timberg, "Hu Defends China's Role in Africa," *Washington Post*, February 8, 2007.

20 Colum Lynch, "China Filling Void Left by West in UN Peacekeeping," *Washington Post*, November 24, 2006.

21 Orville Schell, "What China Needs Now is the World's Respect," *Newsweek*, February 19, 2007.

22 "Jody Williams and Mia Farrow, 'Sudan's Enablers'," *Wall Street Journal*, May 23, 2007.

23 Edward Cody, "Chinese Official Decries Attempts to Link Darfur, Olympics," *Washington Post*, May 19, 2007.

24 Lydia Polgreen and Warren Hoge, "Sudan Relents on Peacekeepers in Darfur," *New York Times*, June 13, 2007.

25 Edward Cody, "In China, a Display of Resolve on Darfur," *Washington Post*, September 16, 2007.

26 "China Seeks to Block UN Report on Darfur, Diplomats Say," *Reuters*, October 19, 2010.

27 Mandy Turner, "The Continuing Scramble for Africa," *The Guardian*, May 2, 2007.

28 Edward Cody, "In China, a Display of Resolve on Darfur," *Washington Post*, September 16, 2007.

29 "Africa Command: US Strategic Interests and the Role of the US Military in Africa," CRS Report, July 6, 2007, available at http://www.fas.org/sgp/crs/natsec/RL34003.pdf. Also see Walter Pincus, "US Africa Command Brings New Concerns," *Washington Post*, May 28, 2007.

30 Michael A. Fletcher, "Bush has Quietly Tripled Aid to Africa," *Washington Post*, December 31, 2006.

31 Alex Perry, "Africa's Oil Dreams," *Time*, May 31, 2007.

32 Craig Whitlock, "North Africa Reluctant to Host US Command," *Washington Post*, June 24, 2007.

33 Paul McLeary, "A Different Kind of Great Game," *Foreign Policy*, March 2007.

7 China and the EU

1 "Engaging China," speech by Sir Leon Brittain, Vice President of the European Commission at the EU–China Academic Network Annual Conference, London, February 2, 1998, available at http://europa.eu.int/rapid/start/cgi/guesten.ksh?p_action.gettxt=gt&doc=SPEECH/98/21101AG.

2 They were laid out in the European Commission's 1998 communication titled "Building a Comprehensive Partnership with China," which is available at http://ec.europa.eu/comm/external_relations/china/com_98/index.htm.

3 See the Joint Statement of the Ninth EU–China Summit of September 10, 2006, available at http://www.gov.cn/misc/2006-09/10/content_383505.htm.

4 Detailed statistics are available at http://ec.europa.eu/ trade/issues/bilateral/countries/china/index_en_htm.

5 Tang Shaocheng, "EU's Taiwan Policy in Light of its China Policy," *Asia Europe Journal*, Vol. 1 (2003), p. 516.

6 See the European Commission's Country Strategy Paper for China that sets out the framework for EU's cooperation with China during the period 2002–2006, available at http://ec.europa.eu/comm/ external_relations/china/csp/02_06en.pdf.

7 Peter Ford, "Ahead of Olympics, China Lifts Foreign Media Restrictions," *The Christian Science Monitor*, December 1, 2006.

8 For details see China's EU Policy Paper of October 2003, available at http://www.fmprc.gov.cn/eng/zxxx/t27708.htm.

9 "EU Urges China to Open Up Or Risk Trade Backlash," *Reuters*, October 25, 2006.

10 Liz Alderman, "Looking for Investments, China Turns to Europe," *New York Times*, November 1, 2010.

11 Ibid.

12 On Europe's view of the world and its divergence from American approach, see Robert Kagan, "Power and Weakness," *Policy Review*, June–July 2002, available at http://www.hoover.org/publications/ policyreview/3460246.html.

13 Sushma Ramachandran, "The Expanding EU–India Relationship," *The Hindu* (Chennai), July 5, 2005.

14 R.K. Jain, "The Pale Continent," available at http://cms.ifa.de/ fileadmin/content/publikationen/kulturreport/fremdbild_jain_e.pdf.

15 Timothy Garton Ash, "The view from Beijing tells you why we need a Europen foreign policy," Guardian, November 10, 2010.

Index

Abe, Shinzo, 25, 27
Ad hoc decision-making, 64
Admiral Gorshkov, 62–63
Advanced Technology Vehicle
    (ATV), 63
advanced weapons technology, 66, 71
Afghanistan, 29, 34, 36, 61, 66
Afghan mujahideen, aid to, 34
Africa, 2–3, 5, 7, 48, 51, 59, 61,
    81–89, 91–93
    aid policies towards, 87
AFRICOM, 92
al-Ahdab oil field of Iraqi, 71
Airborne Warning and Control
    System, 31
Akula II nuclear attack submarine, 63
Andaman and Nicobar Islands, 61
anti-China policies of US, 15
anti-Maoist ideological, 46
anti-ship cruise missiles, 24, 73
Arabian Sea, 33
Arunachal Pradesh, 18–20
ASEAN+3 arrangement, 16
ASEAN Free Trade Agreement, 15
Asia-Europe Meeting (ASEM), 97
Asian Development Bank, 18
Asia-Pacific
    balance of power in, 11–16
    counterbalancing coalition in, 3
Association of South-East Asian
    Nations (ASEAN), 8, 62
Australia, 14, 16, 24–25, 27, 59, 61
authoritarianism, 6
Awami League, 40–41
Aziz, Abdullah bin Abdul, 75

Bab-el Mandeb (Mandab Strait), 51
Babur cruise missile, 31

Bahrain, 62
bail-out package for Pakistan, 32
ballistic missiles, 53, 74, 76, 80
Bangladesh, 19, 24, 29–30, 37–41, 49,
    55
bank-rolling unsavory regimes, 87
al-Bashir, Omar, 6, 90
Bay of Bengal, 33, 40, 54–55, 61, 63
2008 Beijing Olympics, 47, 70, 91
bilateral relationship, 22, 27, 38, 95
Bilateral trade, 39, 43, 75
Bison aircrafts, 24
Britain, 35, 51, 81, 91
Burma, 19, 33, 54–55, 61, 69
Bush, George W., 90
Bush Administration, 12, 23

Chashma Nuclear Power Reactor, 32
chimera of "Chimerica", 14
China–Africa relations
    double aid and interest-free loans to
        Africa, 84
    Forum on China–Africa
        Cooperation, 81
    humanitarian and development aid
        to Africa, 92
    trade, 84, 87
China–Arab Forum, 78
China–Bangladesh, Energy coopera-
    tion between, 39
China–EU relations. *See* EU–China
    relations
China National Nuclear Corporation,
    32
China National Offshore Oil
    Corporation (CNOOC), 85
China National Petroleum
    Corporation (CNPC), 85

China–Nepal, Friendship Treaty, 48
China–Pakistan relations
  all-weather friendship, 19
  collusion on nuclear issues, 30
  counter-terror cooperation between, 34
Chinas National Reform and Development Commission, 73
China Study Centers (CSCs), 47
Chinese intrusions into Indian territory, 18
Christian Aid, 88
climate change, 9, 15, 17, 70, 97
Clinton, Hillary, 7, 16
Cold War, 5, 13, 45–46, 51–52, 58, 67–68, 83, 94, 101
Container Security Initiative (CSI), 60
crucial 'rare earth' minerals, export restrictions, 3
cruise missile, 9, 31, 39, 74
cyber-security and internet freedom, 15
cyber warfare, 24

Dalai Lama, 22, 99
Daqing oilfield, 69
defense budget, 21, 52
Defense Cooperation Agreement, 38
Dingli, Shen, 1
diplomatic aggressiveness, 29
domestic economic development, 5
Domestic political constraints, 21
double-digit growth, 6, 68, 82

economic and military prowess, 2
Economic cooperation, 17
economic co-operation zone in Zambia, 89
economic crisis, 32
economic development program, 66
economic globalization, forces of, 11
economic interactions between China and Nepal, 46
  duty-free access to Nepali goods, 47
economic modernization, 50
EEC–China-Trade and Cooperation agreement, 97

EEC–China Trade and Economic Co-operation Agreement, 95
Eelam War, 44
El Dorado, 81
Equator Principles, 87
EU–China, 94–103
  bilateral trade, 96
  limits to EU–China partnership, 98
  partnership, 101
  relations, 95, 99
  strategic partnership, 96
exclusive economic zone, 16, 43, 57
  FDI, 4

F-16 fighters, 24
financial crisis, 4, 84, 100
Foreign Affairs, 23
foreign currency reserves, 6
foreign policy, 1, 5, 7, 12, 18, 23, 33–34, 38, 41, 47, 49–50, 59, 66, 68–69, 83–85, 95, 97, 102–103
France, 35, 62, 81–82, 91, 101
Free Trade Area, 27
Friendship Treaty, 45, 48
Funabashi, Yoichi, 4

G-2, 13–14
G-3, 14
GDP, 4, 69
genocidal civil war in Darfur, 90
geo-political rivalry, 68
global hegemony, competition with US, 12
Google, 15
GPS-blocking technology, 53
"great power," tag, 93
Gulf of Aden, 20, 56–57
Gwadar Deep-Sea Port, 32–33, 40, 54–55, 61
  concern for India, 33, 36, 55
  funded by China, 32, 61
  "listening post" for China, 36
  strategic location, 55
Gyanendra, King, 46

Hainan Island, 54
Hambantota Development Zone, 43, 55

Han Chinese vs. Muslim Uighurs, 36
Hasina, Sheikh, 41
Herzog, Chaim, 77
Hezbollah, 73, 79–80
Hong Kong, 95, 97
122-mm Howitzers, rocket launchers, 39
Hussein, Saddam, 71

India
  exclusive defense service provider, 62
  largest trading partner — China, 17
  organizational changes in the armed forces of, 63
  procurement delays in major weapon systems, 64
India and Japan, 25–28
India and US, 23–25
  bilateral engagement, 23
  bilateral naval exercises, 24
  Bush Administration, 23
  civilian nuclear energy cooperation pact, 23
  Clinton Administration, 23
  defense cooperation, 24
  non-proliferation, 23
Indian foreign policy, 22–23, 48, 57
Indian Ocean, 2–3, 18, 23, 36, 42, 49, 51–65
  checkpoints, 53, 57
  Chinese agreement with Sri Lanka to access, 55
  Chinese diplomatic and military effort, 55
  Chinese dominance, 49, 54
  diplomatic and military efforts, 55
  diplomatic initiatives, 60–62
  Exclusive Economic Zone of India, 57
  geographical advantage for India, 56
  Hambantota Development Zone, 55
  Indian dominance, 57–58
  Naval platforms, 62–64
  policing of Indian Navy, 62
  power projection capabilities, 3

pre-eminent maritime power, 58
projection of India's naval power, 59–60
role in Indian security, 57
seaborne trade, 51
Security of, 23
Sino-Indian relations, 65
Sino-Indian ties, 2
trade routes, 2
US–Indian maritime cooperation, 36, 55
US–Soviet rivalry, 52
"zone of peace", 52
India–Pakistan peace talks, "blank check" to intervene, 34
India's "Look East" policy, 27, 61
India's defense modernization program, 64
India's naval power projection of into Indian Ocean, 59
India's United Nations Security Council membership, 19
Indonesia, 7, 24, 62
Indo-Sri Lankan agreement of 1987, 41
industrial revolution, 7
INS Jalashwa, 60
Intellectual Property Rights (IPR), 96, 101
interest-free loans to Sri Lanka, 43
International Donors Conference for Palestine, 78
International Monetary Fund (IMF), 15, 32, 85, 87
inter-service rivalry, 64
Inter-Services Intelligence (ISI), 34, 38
Iran, 3, 33, 36, 55, 61, 66–67, 70, 72–80, 99
  missile guidance equipment, 73
  natural gas, 73
  nuclear ambitions, 2
  nuclear program, 73–74
  second-largest oil producer, 73
  Security Council resolutions, 74
  Yadavaran oilfield, 73
Islamist extremism, 34, 36, 72, 81

Israel, 60, 66–67, 71, 73, 76–79
diplomatic closeness with China, 77
HARPY drones (unmanned
aircraft), 77
Oslo agreements, 78
Phalcon early warning aircraft, 77
Sino-Israeli trade, 76
Israeli–Palestinian conflict, 66
Israel–Lebanon conflict, 60

JF-17 fighter aircraft, 31
J-10 fighter jet, 31
Jamaat-ud-Dawa (JuD), 34
Japan, 2–4, 11–17, 22, 24–28, 43, 48,
52, 60–61, 69, 101
Japanese-American rivalry, 65
Jintao, Hu, 30, 61, 77
Joint military exercises, 7

Kashmir, 14, 23, 30–31, 33–34, 36
Khan, Abdul Qadeer, 32
Khusab reactor, 32
Kissinger, Henry, 30
Kunming Initiative, 40
Kuwait, 62, 92

land-attack cruise missiles, 24
land-based ballistic missile, 8
Lashkar-e-Toiba (LeT), 34
Law of the Seas, 57
Liberation Tigers of Tamil Eelam
(LTTE), 41–44
Liberia, 84, 89, 99
Libya, 36
Line of Actual Control (LAC), 18, 37
Line of Actual Control in Arunachal
Pradesh and Sikkim, 18
"Look East" policy, 27

Macau, 95, 97
Mahan, Alfred, 57
Malaysia, 7, 16, 62
Mbeki, Thabo, 87–88, 88
Mearsheimer, John, 2
merchant shipping, 57
Middle East policy, 70–72
arms, 71
energy, 70

Islamic linkage, 72
politics and diplomacy, 71
priorities in the, 66–67
MiG-27, 24
MiG-29, 24
Milhollin, Gary, 31
military expenditures, 1, 52
military modernization, 8–9, 24, 31,
66, 69, 76
Mirage-2000, 24
Missile Technology Control Regime
(MTCR), 76
Monroe Doctrine, 29
Mugabe, Robert, 6, 86
Mugabe's "Look East" policy, 86
multipolar systems, 12
Musharraf, General Pervez, 38
Myanmar, 29, 37, 40, 97, 99

Nanjing incident, 26
NATO countries, 25
Nehru, Jawaharlal, 29
"neo-colonialism,", 85
Nepal, 19, 24, 29–30, 38, 45–49
Netanyahu, Benjamin, 77
New Zealand, 16, 27
non-aligned foreign policy, 58
non-proliferation, 14, 23, 80
North Korea, 15, 36, 69
North Korean and Iranian nuclear
issues, 15
nuclear non-proliferation, 94
Nuclear Non-Proliferation Treaty
(NPT), 31
nuclear proliferation, 9, 74
nuclear submarines, 53, 63
Nuclear Suppliers Group (NSG), 35

Obama, 9, 13–14, 18
Obama Administration, 9, 14, 18
Old Burma Road. See Stilwell Road
Olmert, Ehud, 77
Oman, 62
one China principle, 83
Organization of Petroleum Exporting
Countries (OPEC), 75
Oslo agreements, 78

Pacific and Atlantic Oceans, 51
Pakistan, 14, 19, 23, 29–38, 40–42,
    48–50, 54–56, 58, 69
Pakistan-Occupied Kashmir, 32
Pakistan's military modernization, 31
Pakistan's nuclear weapons program,
    32
Pannikar, K.M., 57
Partnership and Cooperation
    Agreement, 95
patrol aircraft to the Seychelles, 61
Pax Americana, 12
peacekeeping force, 89–91
People's Liberation Army (PLA), 7, 8,
    53, 69
Peoples Republic of China (PRC), 67
PetroChina, 85
Philippines, 7, 16
piracy, 1, 23, 57, 62
Poland, 100
political liberalization, 3
political moderation, 50
post-Cold War international system,
    11
Powell, Colin, 60
Power imbalances, 13
power politics, 9, 37
power projection capabilities, 3
power transition theory, 13
Prabhakaran, Velupillai, 42
Prachanda, Maoist leader, 47–48
pre-eminent maritime power, 58
pro-active naval posture, 58
project an image of a peace-loving, 93
Proliferation Security Initiative (PSI),
    60

Qatar, 62

Rabin, Yitzhak, 77
radicalism of impotence, 5
Rajapaksa, Mahinda, 42–44
revolutionary Communism, 67
Rice, Condoleezza, 23
Rudd, Kevin, 14

satellite-guided missiles, 24
Saudi Arabia, 62, 66–67, 70, 72–73,
    75–76, 79–80, 82, 92
ARAMCO, 75
    biggest oil supplier, 75
SINOPEC, 75
seaborne trade, 51
Sea Lanes of Communication
    (SLOCs), 52
second-largest consumer of oil, China,
    82
Shah, Prithvi Narayan, 45
Shaheen-1 ballistic missile, 31
Shanghai Cooperation Organization
    (SCO), 9, 43
Sharon, Ariel, 77
Shijie, Wang, 78
ship-borne anti-missile defenses, 24
shipping lanes, 7, 16
Singapore, 24, 41, 62
Sino-Bangladeshi bilateral relation-
    ship, 41
Sino-Bangladesh relations, 40
Sino-Indian frictions, 18
Sino-Indian naval competition, 56
Sino-Indian relations, 18, 33, 50, 65
Sino-Indian strategic rivalry, 19
Sino-Indian ties, 2, 20, 33, 56
1962 Sino-Indian war, 30
Sino-Iranian defense, 74
Sino-Iranian relationship, 74
Sino-Japanese tensions, 4, 26
Sino-Pakistani relation, 34
Sino-Pakistan ties, 2, 30–37
SINOPEC, 75
Sino-Saudi relationship, 75
Sino-Sri Lankan bilateral relationship,
    41
Sino-US relations, 3, 67
smuggling, 62
South Asian Association for Regional
    Cooperation (SAARC), 39
South China Sea, 7–9, 16, 25, 54–55,
    62
"Southern Tibet". *See* Arunachal
    Pradesh
space monitoring post in Mongolia, 61
space weapons, 24
splendid isolation, policy of, 29
Spratly Islands, ownership of, 7

Sri Lanka, 24, 29–30, 38, 41–44, 49, 55
Stern, Todd, 15
Stilwell Road, 40
STOBAR Air Defense Ship, 62
Strait of Hormuz, 32, 36, 51, 55, 57
Strait of Malacca, 51, 55, 57, 61
strategic environment in the Asia-Pacific, 13, 27
Strategic Priorities, 68–70
    economics and energy, 68–69
    military, 69
    political, 69–70, 69
string of pearls strategy, 54, 59
Su-30, 24
Sudan, 69, 82, 84–86, 88–91, 99
Suez Canal, 51, 57
surface-to-air missiles, 8, 24

Taiwan, 6–7, 9, 14–16, 21, 24–25, 27, 31, 41, 53, 67, 69–70, 83, 99
    diplomatic recognition to, 6, 77, 83
    export-dependent economy, 16
    reunification, 99
Taiwan Straits, 9, 21
Taliban, 14
Tamil Tigers, 44
terror attack in Mumbai, November 2008, 18, 34
Theatre-range ballistic missiles, 24
Third World, 5, 67–68, 83
threats to sea-lanes, 62
Tiananmen Square, massacre in, 71
Tibet, 16, 22, 31, 41, 45–48, 70, 99
Tibetan refugees, 46
Todd Stern, 15
tourism, 95, 102
Trade between China and Africa, 84
trade surplus, 4, 6
trans-Atlantic partnership, 101

Uighur insurgency, 72
undervalued currency, 3
United Arab Emirates, 62
United Nations, 6, 27, 60, 73–74, 82, 86, 89–91, 101
United Nations peacekeepers, 90
United Nations Security Council, 27, 73–74, 89, 91
United States, 9, 17, 25, 27, 29, 34, 45–46, 48, 66, 70, 76, 97, 100–101, 103
UN Security Council, 70, 91, 99
    China's veto, 99
US–India relations
    bilateral ties, 60
    civilian nuclear energy cooperation pact, 18
    maritime cooperation, 36, 55
    nuclear pact, 19, 35
    partnership, 20
US–Japan relationship, 15
US military power in Afghanistan and Iraq, 12
US Navy, 8

Vietnam, 7–8, 16, 62
Vietnam War, 8

WMD proliferation, 25
Wolfowitz, Paul, 87
World Bank, 85, 87
World Economic Forum, 15
World Trade Organization (WTO), 96, 100–101
    trade disputes, 100
World War II, 15, 26

Xiaoping, Deng, 5

Yadavaran oilfield, 73
Yellow Sea, 8, 16

al-Zahar, Mahmud, 78
Zanganeh, Bijan Namdar, 73
Zardari, Asif Ali, 30, 34
Zhuhai Zhenrong Corporation, 73
Zimbabwe, 85–86, 88–89, 99
"zone of peace". See Indian Ocean